Acknowledgements

Thanks first to Tim Tucker, Bodie McDowell and Charles Frank, who embraced the idea. And of course, thanks to Charlie Flood for the inspiration when it was needed and the means to carry it out.

Thanks to the state chairmen who busted their buns to meet a tight schedule: Bob Kornegay, Roy Edwards, Bodie McDowell, Tom Pearce, Jim Casada, Horace Carter, John and Denise Phillips and Ann Taylor.

Thanks to the multi-talented Cliff Shelby for the artwork and to Soc Clay for the cover photo. And to Tim Tucker again and John Allen Smith for the other photos.

Thanks to the storytellers: Horace Carter, Tom Rollins, Tim Mead, Jim Casada, Bob Kornegay again, Pete Cooper, Ed Vice, Sam Roberson and Jim Ritchie, a newcomer.

Thanks to our sages: Charley Dickey, Charlie Elliott, and the late Archibald Rutledge.

And to Ellen Rolfes of The Wimmer Companies, who put it all together.

And especially to The One Who Made It All!

Recipes from the following cookbooks and/or agencies have been used:

Jennewein-Nesbitt-Kilburn Kitchens, Wrightsville, North Carolina
Living off the Land...Thomas K. Squier
Recipes of the Wild...National Wild Turkey Federation, Inc.
Saltwater Fishing with Dr. Jim...James C. Wright, MD, Virginia Beach, Virginia
Savor the Wild...NAHC Wild Game Cookbook

Horse's Overs

*T*hat's how one of my buddies, who lacked a whole lot of formal education, used to pronounce hors d'oeuvres. Y'all know what I'm talking about: the stuff you eat before you really sit down to eat. Well, these few paragraphs must be digested before you get to the really good stuff, though they'd no doubt be much more palatable with the crab dip found a few pages over.

When we all get to Heaven, it will be revealed unto us that men go to camp to eat. Casting a bait or calling a turkey or pulling a trigger: all these things are simply Rules of the Chase. The real reason for The Call of the Wild comes when the catch is introduced to the fire.

Since the day when Early Man tasted the first brontosaurus-burger grilled over a lightning-struck tree, the human race has steadily moved upward on the evolutionary scale, outdistancing those other predators which have never perfected the skill of cooking their prey. Man, the ultimate predator, may nowadays still grill his catch over a primitive fire or microwave it in the latest space-age technological fashion—yet he no longer eats simply to sustain life; he does it because it TASTES GOOD!

The Good Lord has given mankind a bountiful buffet in the bosom of Mother Nature and modern research is now proving that wild game is more healthful than domesticated tablefare, in most cases. Having said that, let me make it clear that no outdoorsman worth his salt will admit to eating anything simply because it is good for him. We eat game, fish and outdoor stuff because (1) we enjoy it and (2) it is outdoors. If it just happens to be healthy to boot, well, that's merely icing on the cake. We can't be blamed for it.

In putting this book together, we tried for great recipes of most species of Southern game and fish, to be prepared in modern kitchens. However, there are also scattered amongst these formal dinner table concoctions, a few of the primitive campfire secrets of savor, tested by countless trips afield with old friends.

After all, the friendships formed around the fires could hardly stand the test of time if the cooking wasn't good.

So, pull up a log, fix a toddy, see if you think that barbecued bass ain't the best you ever put in your mouth and lemme tell you a story about the time me and Dude got caught in that ice storm. It was thundering to beat the band and hail was coming down like marbles...

Robert Hitt Neill

Table of Contents

Definitions and Disclaimers
(or How Many Sploots to a Gullop?)

Seems like the easiest thing in the world would be to get a bunch of professional outdoorsmen to send in their favorite game and fish recipes for a cookbook. Being a professional outdoorsman myself, I hied me off to the backyard to knock out my Famous Award-Winning Duck Shish-Ka-Bob Recipe before the rush started. Since I had never written it down, I asked Betsy to tag along and make the notes while I whipped up the sauce, which is the key to the whole thing.

"Okay, about six sploots of Wooster..."

"What's a 'sploot'?"

"That's a pretty hard shake," I declared. "Now, you..."

"So how many tablespoons or teaspoons are in a sploot? And exactly how many sploots do you use? And what's a 'pretty hard shake'? You have to be specific when you write a recipe!"

Point is, most men cook "by the seat of their britches" as the saying goes, and test by taste. To put this book together required more patience in more states than anything since the Confederate Constitution and our womenfolk are to be commended for their diligence in getting the measurements down on paper.

But when cooking by taste, the recipe is subject to the seasonings that the cook likes and that differs with the territory, in many cases. What Butch Thumond from South Louisiana likes may be a heckuva lot hotter than what Bubba Garitta from North Carolina enjoys. Bear that in mind.

Jim Ritchie writes of the family cook revealing the recipe for molasses cookies, which included three "gullops" of molasses. When queried as to the exact amount of a gullop, her answer was, "you just throws the jug over your arm and pour. It says 'gullop, gullop, gullop' and you cuts it off."

Dude McElwee's prescription for the coffee at the nightly campfire includes a "dollop" of Kahlúa, not to be in any way confused with a "gullop" if you plan to hunt the next morning.

In other words, dear cooks, while most of these recipes are tried and true, and have been tested and fine-tuned for years around hunting camps and hunters' kitchens, many had never been actually measured scientifically before. They are designed to be enjoyed just as much by the cook as by the diners and we encourage tasting as you go. Add a whiff of woodsmoke, a dollop of this, a sploot of that, a gullop or two and a pinch—even if the latter is applied to someone of the opposite sex wandering too close to the fire. That's the spirit of these concoctions, and they're supposed to be fun to both cook and eat. Take these suggestions with our recipes—and make them your own favorites!

Robert Hitt Neill

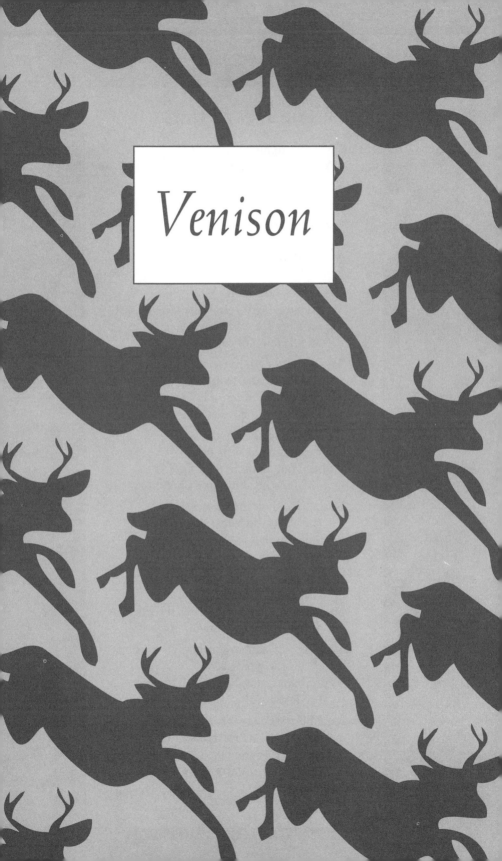

Venison

The Deer Hunt

I'm sitting in my deer stand
    high in the old oak tree.
Waiting now for daylight
    anxious as can be.

My arrow's loaded in my bow
    in eagerness I wait.
Wondering what this day will bring
    and what shall be my fate.

Golden rays of sunlight
    are piercing through the trees.
Lighting up the landscape
    and dancing off the leaves.

The woods begin to waken
    and life begins to stir.
When out the corner of my eye
    I catch a brown-gray blur.

It is a deer, so silent now
    that I can't hear its tread.
It's been out all night feeding
    and now heading for its bed.

Graceful as a ballerina
    she walks the forest floor.
Reminiscent of an eagle
    as it sets its wings to soar.

Her ears come up, her nose held high
    she senses something's wrong.
She turns and looks and paws the earth,
    and now I see the fawn.

Slipping and skulking through the woods
    they slowly fade away.
As do visions of a shot
    I've lost my chance today.

But I'll be back another time
    again to take this stand
For success is in the being there
    and not what's brought to hand.

Bob Anderson

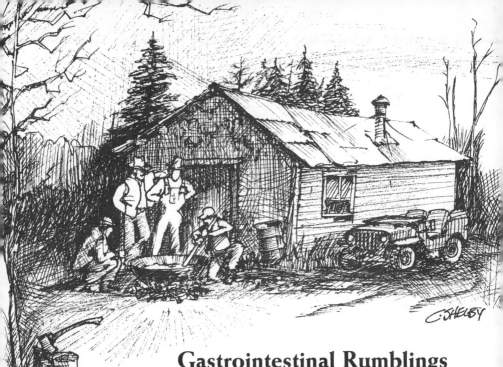

Gastrointestinal Rumblings

*T*he best outdoor meal I ever ate will never be exactly duplicated. It won't be duplicated for the simple reason that nobody knows exactly what went into it. It was a pure community project with contributions from everyone who wished to participate. It didn't start out that way but that's the way it turned out. And it was, as the saying goes, indescribably delicious.

We were at deer camp and someone decided that we should scour out the old wash pot that had been sitting in the middle of camp for years and which nobody could find a good use for, since things are not usually washed at deer camp. Clothes or people. Then, once the pot was relatively free of the mysterious residue which had accumulated on it, we could make a stew. Some of us thought that was a good idea (that night, after all the toasts to the deer, dogs, outdoor life, rifles, shotguns, Ducks Unlimited and the Methodist Church, among other things, ANYTHING would have been a good idea), so we bustled around and hit the pot a few licks with some SOS pads to make it presentable...maybe not presentable to the Pure Food and Drug Act folks, but it looked okay to us. Willie, the camp helper, did most of the work, since he had not participated too heavily in the toasting session.

We filled the pot about half full of water, built a fire around it and when the water boiled, we began the scientific act of adding the ingredients. Some potatoes went in along with canned tomatoes, lots of salt and pepper, some of last year's celery salt that someone's wife had brought to camp on a fishing trip and other things like that. We added a few pounds of deer meat, a squirrel or two, a duck or two, a couple of what was purported to be quail and other things like that. Then we made sure that we had enough wood stacked around the pot to last the night and went to bed.

The next morning, before we took up stands, we checked the stew and it was doing fine. One of the pseudo cooks, who had been one of the main toasters the night before and who had at least temporarily sworn off toasting, poured a fifth of Jack Daniels Black Label in "to give it a little twang." A couple of real dyed-in-the-wool hunters, who had passed on the toasting session and who had killed a 'coon and a 'possum the night before, added these prizes to the stew that morning. Then we stacked enough wood around the pot to last the morning and went deer hunting.

We came in around noon to rest up and get ready for the afternoon hunt and to check on the stew. It was still roiling and boiling and doing great. After a taste or two by a bunch of folks, we began to fine tune the taste. Some onions, hot sauce, a rabbit, meat tenderizer and a few more twang ingredients were added. The stew had boiled down to where everything in it was pretty nondescript in a kind of mush. The bubbles that pushed up through all that stuff popped in a kind of meaty "blup." A statement was made that somebody could fall in that stew and be forever unaccounted for. Then somebody hollered for Willie to get more wood. No Willie. That was not like him not to be around when you needed him. The thought occurred to all of us at the same time that Willie was "unaccounted for." All eyes went to the stew.

"Blup...blup."

Nobody said anything but we all dispersed in a hell of a hurry to look for Willie and happily somebody found him asleep over by the skinning rack. A piece of wire mesh from the dog pen area was hurriedly put over the pot to satisfy any OSHA requirements and we stacked enough wood around the pot to keep it going through the afternoon and went back to the woods.

After we returned from the afternoon hunt, tired, cold, wet from a light all-afternoon drizzle and hungry enough to eat the hind end out of a rag doll, we decided that the stew was ready and we ate it. All of it. And if I had the exact recipe for that stew, my balance sheet would look better than IBM's. I have eaten in some multi-star restaurants all over the country but I have never tasted anything that even remotely could measure up to that. I mean it was outstanding! And it gets better as the years go by.

My belly doctor told me shortly thereafter that I had an ulcer. But I'm not blaming the stew. Nothing that good could cause an ulcer.

Jim Ritchie
Shocco, Mississippi
from *Shocco Tales: Southern Fried Sagas*

Bill Miller's Roast Venison

1	(8 to 10 pound) venison roast
	Salt and black pepper
1	apple, peeled and sliced
1	envelope dry onion soup mix
½	cup warm water
	Worcestershire sauce
½	cup water
	Barbecue sauce (optional)

Trim all fat from roast. Season with salt and pepper. Place in roasting pan. Arrange apple slices on top of roast. Mix soup mix with just enough warm water to form paste; spread over apples. Sprinkle with Worcestershire sauce. Add ½ cup water to roasting pan. Bake, covered, at 250 degrees for 6 to 7 hours, adding water as necessary to keep roast from sticking to pan. Check for doneness. Discard pan liquid and apples. Serve roast as an entree with barbecue sauce or cut into small pieces for appetizer servings.

Roast may be cooked in electric skillet; cooking time may be less than 6 to 7 hours.

Yield: 14 to 18 servings

Charley Dickey
Tallahassee, Florida

Grilled Venison

1	(6 to 8 pound) deer shoulder or ham
1	tablespoon salt
1	tablespoon black pepper
1	tablespoon garlic salt
5 or 6	slices bacon

Trim all fat from shoulder or ham. Rub salt, pepper and garlic salt into surface of meat. Wrap bacon slices around meat. Place on large aluminum foil rectangle and wrap to form tight package. Chill unfrozen meat overnight in refrigerator; store frozen meat in refrigerator for 24 hours. Cook on gas grill over low heat for 2½ hours.

Yield: 8 to 10 servings

Dottie Burkhart
Lexington, North Carolina

Venison Pot Roast

¼	cup all-purpose flour
¼	cup firmly packed brown sugar
1	teaspoon paprika
½	teaspoon black pepper
1	(3 to 5 pound) venison rump or shoulder
6	tablespoons butter
½	cup venison or beef broth
2	stalks celery, chopped
1	onion, chopped
10	onions, quartered (optional)
10	potatoes, quartered (optional)

Blend flour, brown sugar and seasoning; sprinkle over meat. Saute meat in butter in Dutch oven, turning to brown all sides. Add broth, celery and chopped onion. Bake, covered, at 375 degrees for 3½ to 4 hours, adding onions and potatoes to bake during the final 30 minutes.

Other good vegetables to serve with the roast are yellow squash casserole, duck camp celery and spiced carrots.

Yield: 10 to 12 servings

Uncle Russ Chittenden
Paducah, Kentucky

Venison and Apples

	Vegetable oil
4	venison steaks
4	apples, sliced

Pour just enough oil in large cast iron skillet to moisten the bottom. Heat until smoking. Add steaks and sear both sides. Reduce heat. Drop in sliced apples, arranging to completely cover steaks. Cook, tightly covered, for 30 to 40 minutes or until steaks are fork tender.

Red Delicious apples maintain their shape during cooking. Onions may be substituted for apples. Boiled potatoes or cabbage are good side dishes with the venison.

Yield: 4 servings

Sam Roberson
Lobelville, Tennessee

Blackened Venison

Humberto Fontova believes this is "the best venison you'll ever eat...puts roast venison to shame." He prefers cuts from yearlings and doesn't use deer older than 2½ years.

Venison backstrap or haunch
Garlic powder
Meat tenderizer
Freshly ground black pepper
Extra virgin olive oil
Butter

Cut venison into ¾-inch thick steaks. Sprinkle with seasonings. Pound lightly to roughen surface and imbed seasonings. Place mixture of oil and butter in bottom of cast iron skillet and heat to smoking over propane burner. Add steaks; avoid spatters. Blacken on each side.

Humberto Fontova
Covington, Louisiana

Southern Steaks

2½	pounds venison, cut in 2-inch pieces
3	tablespoons vinegar
¾	teaspoon salt
1	teaspoon black pepper
½	cup butter
¾	cup water

Pound venison pieces with rolling pin. Combine vinegar, salt and pepper; rub into both sides of venison. Saute pieces quickly in butter in skillet, turning to brown on both sides. Add water and cook, covered, to desired tenderness.

Yield: 6 servings

Elise Vachon
Marietta, Georgia

Venison Steak

4	slices bacon
½	large onion, chopped
1	tablespoon sugar
10	(1 inch thick) venison steak cutlets from backstrap
	Juice of 1 lemon
	Lemon pepper

Fry bacon in cast iron skillet. Remove slices from pan, leaving 2 tablespoons drippings in skillet and reserve remaining grease. Add onion to drippings and sprinkle with sugar; cook until onion is tender. Remove onion and return reserved grease to skillet. Place cutlets in skillet; squeeze small amount of lemon juice on each and season with lemon pepper. Cook quickly; meat is best if cutlets are still slightly pink in the center. Add crumbled bacon and onion to cutlets and reheat. Serve immediately.

Wild rice is a good accompaniment to cutlets.

Yield: 3 to 4 servings

Jim and Ann Casada
Rock Hill, South Carolina

Venison Wisconsin

Venison tenderloin or butterfly (½ inch thick) steaks from rump
Butter
Salt and black pepper to taste
Burgundy wine
Brandy

Sear steaks quickly in butter, seasoning with salt and pepper. Add wine and simmer for a few minutes, cooking steaks to medium doneness. Remove steaks from pan, add brandy to pan liquid and warm briefly. Pour over steaks and ignite to serve flambe.

Good side dishes include potatoes au gratin and green beans with bits of bacon and onion.

Bill Schulz
Atlanta, Georgia

Deer Island Delight

2	cups chopped green onion
5	cloves garlic, minced
¼	cup firmly packed brown sugar
¼	teaspoon ground ginger
2	tablespoons cornstarch
1½	cups water
¾	cup soy sauce
1	cup dry sherry
2½ to 3	pounds venison steak, boned and cut in strips
2	pounds uncooked white rice
1½	pounds broccoli, cut in flowerets
1	red bell pepper, sliced
1	pound carrots, sliced
½	pound fresh mushrooms, sliced
¾	cup vegetable oil

Combine onion, garlic, brown sugar, ginger, cornstarch, water, soy sauce and sherry. Add venison strips and chill, covered, for 1 to 2 hours. Prepare rice according to package directions, cooking while preparing meat with vegetables. Remove meat from marinade, reserving 1 cup liquid. Stir fry meat strips and vegetables in large wok or skillet over high heat, cooking until meat is done and vegetables are tender. Add reserved marinade and heat thoroughly. Serve over hot rice.

Marinade time may be shortened for less intense flavor.

Yield: 10 servings

Howard P. Lindsey
Bowling Green, Kentucky

Sowhatchet Country-Fried Venison

¾	cup all-purpose flour, divided
¼	teaspoon garlic salt
1	teaspoon salt
¼	teaspoon black pepper
2 or 3	(1 inch thick) venison round steaks, cut in serving-sized pieces
	Vegetable oil
1	bouillon cube
1	cup hot water
	Bottled brown bouquet sauce
	Dash of Worcestershire sauce

Combine ½ cup flour, garlic salt, salt and pepper; pound flour mixture into both sides of steaks. Sear steaks in oil in heavy skillet; remove from skillet. Retain 3 to 4 tablespoons drippings in skillet. Dissolve bouillon cube in water; set aside. Gradually add ¼ cup flour to drippings; gradually add dissolved bouillon, bouquet sauce and Worcestershire sauce, stirring and cooking until thickened. Add steaks to sauce. Simmer, covered, for 30 minutes.

Yield: 4 to 6 servings

Charley Dickey
Tallahassee, Florida

"Most of our harmless and genuine joys in this life are those which find their source in primitive instincts. A man who follows his natural inclinations, with due deference to common sense and moderation, is usually on the right track. Now the sport of hunting is one of the most honorable of the primeval instincts of man."

Archibald Rutledge

Venison Swiss Steak

3 tablespoons all-purpose flour
1 (2 pound) venison steak, ½ to 1 inch thick
½ cup butter or margarine
1 medium-sized onion, coarsely chopped
1 small green bell pepper, coarsely chopped
1 stalk celery, cut in ¼-inch slices
1 (16 ounce) can peeled tomatoes
2 cups beef consomme or bouillon
1 tablespoon salt
2 crushed peppercorns

Using mallet or edge of saucer, pound flour into both sides of steak. Saute steak in butter in large skillet over high heat, quickly browning both sides. Place vegetables in heavy pot or Dutch oven and arrange steak on vegetables. Add skillet drippings, consomme and seasonings. Simmer, tightly covered, for about 1½ hours or until meat is tender.

Serve Swiss steak with fluffy whipped potatoes, buttered broad noodles or over white rice.

Yield: 4 servings

Uncle Russ Chittenden
Paducah, Kentucky

Flora Mae's Loin Chops

6 (1 inch thick) venison loin chops
Worcestershire sauce
Garlic salt
Salt and black pepper to taste
¼ cup melted butter
Butter
Parsley sprigs for garnish

Trim all fat from chops and wipe with clean damp cloth. Sprinkle each chop with Worcestershire sauce and season with garlic salt, salt and pepper. Saute chops on both sides in melted butter in hot cast iron skillet, then cook, uncovered, over medium heat until chops are done. Serve hot with extra butter on each chop and garnish with parsley.

Yield: 6 servings

Charley Dickey
Tallahassee, Florida

Debbie's Grilled Loin

6   (3x2 inch) venison loin strips
2   tablespoons butter, melted
6   slices bacon
    Salt and black pepper to taste

Baste strips with butter. Wrap each with 1 bacon slice. Grill over medium hot coals, turning frequently, for 4 to 5 minutes on each side for rare and 6 minutes on each side for medium doneness. Season with salt and pepper.

Yield: 5 or 6 servings

Charley Dickey
Tallahassee, Florida

Barbecued Venison Ribs

       Vinegar
       Water
6   pounds venison ribs
2½   teaspoons salt, divided
2   bay leaves
10   peppercorns
1   onion, sliced
1   cup chili sauce
1   cup water
¼   cup steak sauce
½   teaspoon chili powder

Combine vinegar with water in 1:3 proportion in quantity to cover ribs. Add 2 teaspoons salt, bay leaves, peppercorns and onion. Marinate in refrigerator for 2 days. Remove ribs and drain on paper towel. Combine ½ teaspoon salt, chili sauce, 1 cup water, steak sauce and chili powder in saucepan. Bring to a boil, stir and remove from heat. Prepare charcoal to produce medium-hot coals. Brush ribs with sauce and place on grill. Grill for at least 1 hour or until tender, basting every 10 to 15 minutes and turning frequently.

Yield: 4 servings

Tim Tucker
Micanopy, Florida

Monkey's Eyebrow Venison Kebabs

Noting that kebabs are a "good first day in the camp meal," Steve Vaughn says the loin is delicious even if there isn't time to hang and air it for awhile.

2	pounds deer tenderloin, cut in cubes
6	medium-sized onions, quartered
12 to 18	cherry tomatoes
2	large green bell peppers, cut in slices
12 to 18	mushrooms (optional)
1	tablespoon lemon pepper
1	tablespoon garlic salt
1	cup butter, melted

Place venison cubes on 9-inch (or longer) skewers; add onion, tomato, bell pepper and mushrooms; repeat ingredients. Mix lemon pepper and garlic salt with butter. Generously baste kebabs with butter. Place on grill and cook to preferred doneness; 6 to 8 minutes over medium coals produces medium well done meat.

Serve kebabs with green salad and baked potato.

Yield: 4 servings

Steve Vaughn
Paducah, Kentucky

"There is no peace on earth like that of being alone in the deep wilderness, in the glow of a bright campfire."

Charlie Elliott

Marinated Venison

3	pounds shoulder, neck or breast venison
2	medium-sized onions, sliced
1	carrot, sliced
2	stalks celery, chopped
1	clove garlic, crushed
1	teaspoon salt
10	peppercorns
5	juniper berries, crushed
1	tablespoon chopped parsley
1	bay leaf
	Juice of 1 lemon
½	cup vegetable oil
	All-purpose flour
	Water

Remove bones and tough tendons from venison and cut into 1½-inch cubes. Combine vegetables, seasonings, lemon juice and oil in large glass dish. Add meat cubes. Marinate in refrigerator for 1 to 2 days, turning several times. Place meat and marinade in large pot. Gradually bring to a boil, then cook, covered, over low heat for 1½ to 2 hours or until meat is tender. Remove meat. Strain liquid, forcing vegetables through strainer. Thicken pan liquid by adding flour mixed with water. Serve gravy with venison.

Yield: 6 servings

Charley Dickey
Tallahassee, Florida

Bette's Venison Backstrap

10   (1-inch thick) backstrap slices
1   cup herb and spice salad dressing
     Garlic powder
     Hickory smoked salt
¼   cup Burgundy
     Cooked wild rice

Marinate meat in salad dressing in shallow pan for 30 minutes. Remove meat and reserve marinade. Sprinkle meat with garlic powder and smoked salt. Heat iron skillet to hot, reduce heat to medium and add enough marinade to cover bottom of skillet. Place meat slices in skillet, turning quickly to sear each side; cook for 3 to 4 minutes on one side, turn and cook for 4 minutes on other side. Add marinade if necessary to prevent sticking. Add Burgundy, mixing with skillet liquids. Turn meat several times. Transfer meat to heated platter and pour skillet liquid over slices. Serve with wild rice.

Yield: 4 servings

Charley Dickey
Tallahassee, Florida

Wayne's Oven Jerky

Jerky is twice as American as apple pie and ten times more nutritious; it is pure protein and hard as a brickbat. It keeps forever and is ideal concentrated energy on camping trips. Charles Dickey suggests that if you chew on it at the office, people will ask what you're grinding on and that's the perfect opening to tell them how you shot the big buck.

Lean venison strips
Hickory smoked salt
Black pepper

Slice meat with the grain into strips 5 to 6 inches long by ¼ inch wide; trim away any fat membranes. Season with smoked salt and pepper. Chill overnight. Place a large round wooden pick through 1 end of each slice. Using picks as hangers, suspend strips from wire racks in oven. Set oven temperature at 180 degrees and prop door slightly ajar to allow moisture to escape. Drying process should take about 6 hours. Store jerky in plastic bag or jar with screw-top lid; refrigeration is unnecessary if jerky is stored in airtight container.

Do not attempt to speed drying by setting oven temperature higher because meat must be dehydrated rather than cooked.

Charley Dickey
Tallahassee, Florida

Deer Cacciatore

1½	pounds venison, cut in serving-sized pieces
1	cup wine or red vinegar
¼	cup olive oil
	Salt and black pepper to taste
	Vegetable oil
1	pound fresh mushrooms, sliced
3	cloves garlic, minced
1	(16 ounce) can whole tomatoes
¼	cup chopped fresh parsley

Combine wine, oil, salt and pepper in glass dish. Add meat and marinate overnight. Remove meat and reserve marinade. Saute meat in oil in skillet, turning to brown on both sides. Remove from skillet. Saute mushrooms in oil until tender; remove from skillet. Saute garlic. Add meat, tomatoes, parsley, mushrooms and reserved marinade to garlic. Cook over medium heat for about 1 hour or until meat is tender.

Duck may be substituted for venison.

Yield: 4 servings

Terry Silvestri
Branford, Connecticut

Venison Loin

Soy sauce
Venison loin

Marinate loin in soy sauce for at least three hours, overnight if possible. Turn loin occasionally. Cook over medium to hot coals for 20 to 30 minutes, according to your own taste in meat. The soy sauce marinade actually cooks the meat, and all the fire does is warm it up, as far as I am concerned. DO NOT OVERCOOK! Turn loin frequently and baste with the soy sauce. Heat remaining sauce to pour over loin when serving.

Yield: How many this serves depends on how big a deer you killed. If yours are always as big as mine, one loin will serve 6 couples.

Robert Hitt Neill
Brownspur, Mississippi

Venison with Sour Cream

2 pounds venison, cut in 2-inch cubes
1 clove garlic, minced
¼ cup vegetable shortening
1 cup diced celery
½ cup chopped onion
1 cup diced carrots
2 cups water
1 teaspoon salt
Dash of black pepper
1 bay leaf
¼ cup melted butter or margarine
¼ cup all-purpose flour
1 (8 ounce) carton sour cream
Parsley sprigs for garnish

Saute venison and garlic in shortening in skillet over medium heat, turning to brown meat on all sides. Place meat in shallow 2½-quart casserole. Saute celery, onion and carrots in drippings in skillet for 2 minutes. Stir in water and seasonings; pour over venison. Bake at 350 degrees for 30 minutes. Remove from oven and drain, reserving cooking liquid. Combine butter and flour in skillet and cook over low heat, stirring until smooth. Add reserved liquid and cook until thickened, stirring constantly. Stir in sour cream. Pour sauce over venison and vegetables. Garnish with parsley.

Yield: 6 to 8 servings

Charley Dickey
Tallahassee, Florida

Dutch Oven Venison Stew

A complete meal, especially when prepared and started in the middle of the day. After fishing or hunting all afternoon, the stew is ready when you return to camp.

2½ to 3	pounds venison, cubed
½	(8 ounce) bottle ketchup-type steak sauce
1	(8 ounce) bottle steak sauce
	3 tablespoons hot sauce
1	(12 ounce) can warm beer
1	(96 to 117 ounce) can mixed vegetables, drained

Dig shallow hole in ground, deep enough to contain Dutch oven with space around sides for ventilation. Place 2 to 3 pounds charcoal briquettes in hole and ignite. Place meat in Dutch oven. Add sauces, beer and vegetables. When briquettes are white, place about a fourth of them on top of covered Dutch oven and place it over briquettes in hole. Cook for about 4 hours, adding liquid if necessary.

Other vegetables may be substituted for mixed. Use extra charcoal if weather is cold.

Yield: 8 to 10 servings for deer hunters, 14 to 16 servings for "regular people"

Howard P. Lindsey
Bowling Green, Kentucky

Venison Stew

2 pounds venison, cut in 1-inch cubes
¼ cup bacon drippings
Water
1½ teaspoons salt
½ teaspoon black pepper
1 teaspoon garlic salt
1 teaspoon Worcestershire sauce
¾ cup chopped onion
4 medium potatoes, cubed
6 medium carrots, sliced
1 green bell pepper, chopped
2 cups sliced celery
3 tablespoons all-purpose flour
¼ cup cold water

Saute venison in bacon drippings in heavy Dutch oven, turning to brown all sides of meat. Add water to cover, seasonings and onion. Simmer, covered, for about 2 hours. Add vegetables and cook for about 20 minutes or until vegetables are tender. Dissolve flour in ¼ cup water and stir into stew; cook for about 5 minutes. Serve hot.

Yield: 8 servings

Charley Dickey
Tallahassee, Florida

"Few human relationships are closer than those established by a mutual contact with nature; and it has always seemed to me that if more fathers were woodsmen, and would teach their sons to be likewise, most of the so-called father-and-son problems would vanish."

Archibald Rutledge

Cajun Venison Stew

1½	cups chopped onion
1	cup chopped green bell pepper
2	cups (1 inch cubes) carrots
2	cups (1 inch cubes) potatoes
1	cup (1 inch pieces) celery
1	cup diced turnips
1	(8 ounce) can mushrooms, drained
2	pounds venison, cut in cubes
2	(10¾ ounce) cans cream of mushroom soup, undiluted
1½	cups dry red wine
	Salt and black pepper to taste
	Garlic powder or 2 cloves fresh garlic, crushed
1	tablespoon Worcestershire sauce
1 or 2	dashes hot pepper sauce
2	beef-flavored bouillon cubes, crushed
	Water or wine

Layer vegetables in 4 to 6-quart slow-cooker, filling ½ to ⅔ full. Place meat on top of vegetables. Combine soup, wine, seasonings and bouillon; pour over meat and vegetables. Add water or additional wine until liquid is visible around meat. Cook on low setting for 8 hours.

Serve with crusty bread and green salad.

Yield: 4 to 6 servings

Marjorie V. Walworth
Hephzibah, Georgia

Venison Chili

2	pounds venison, finely diced
1	tablespoon bacon drippings
1	teaspoon salt
½	teaspoon black pepper
2	tablespoons chili powder
1	teaspoon sage
1	teaspoon cumin
2	onions, diced
2	cloves garlic, diced
2	(15 ounce) cans Spanish-style tomato sauce
2	cups water
1	(23 ounce) can ranch-style beans

Saute venison in bacon drippings. Add seasonings, onion and garlic. Stir in tomato sauce, water and beans. Simmer for 1 hour.

Serve chili with shredded lettuce, shredded Cheddar cheese, tortilla chips, diced onion and chili powder.

Yield: 6 servings

Charley Dickey
Tallahassee, Florida

Pan-Fried Venison Steaks

Venison steaks
Lemon-Pepper Marinade
¼   pound butter or margarine

Sprinkle steaks on both sides with Lemon-Pepper Marinade. Heat a large cast-iron skillet until hot enough to melt butter, and slice several chunks of butter or margarine into skillet to melt. As soon as butter is melted, drop steaks into skillet. Cook only about a minute on each side, depending of course on the thickness of the steaks; we slice ours about ⅜-inch thick. Do not overcook. Add more chunks of butter as needed to keep the meat from sticking. Serve straight onto your diners' plates from the skillet and keep cooking until you have made all your guests happy campers.

Robert Hitt Neill
Brownspur, Mississippi

Company Chili

3	pounds ground venison
1	pound hot bulk pork sausage
3	medium-sized onions, chopped
2	cloves garlic, minced
½	cup ketchup
¼	cup chili powder
1	teaspoon salt
1	teaspoon black pepper
2	teaspoons ground oregano
2	(29 ounce) cans tomatoes, drained and chopped
3	(16 ounce) cans kidney beans

Combine venison, sausage, onion and garlic in Dutch oven. Cook until meat is browned, stirring to crumble. Drain excess grease. Add ketchup, seasonings and tomatoes. Simmer, covered, for 1 hour, stirring occasionally. Add beans and simmer for additional 30 minutes.

Yield: 10 to 12 servings

Ronnie Strickland
Natchez, Mississippi

Lwt'sai or Camel Drivers' Fare

The story goes that camel drivers crossing wide expanses of the desert used this fare for take-along meals. The mixture can be sealed in a can or glass jar and will last for several days without refrigeration.

1	pound onions, chopped
	Vegetable oil
2	pounds ground venison
1	pound ground pork
1	pound sauerkraut, drained
2	tablespoons soy sauce
1	tablespoon ginger
1	teaspoon red pepper
	Bread slices, buttered on 1 side

Saute onion in oil until translucent. Add venison and pork; fry until thoroughly cooked. Add sauerkraut and cook until well done. Stir in soy sauce and spices. Place 1 slice buttered bread in tostada iron. Spoon meat mixture on bread slice, top with second bread slice and close tostata; trim excess bread from edges. Cook over flame or electric heat until bread is toasted.

Yield: 10 cups

Raymond Moody
Fairhope, Alabama

Cornelius' Venison Liver

6	tablespoons butter or margarine
¼	cup dry white wine
2	large onions, chopped
1	(4 ounce) can sliced mushrooms
8	(⅛ inch thick) slices venison liver
	Salt and black pepper

Melt butter in skillet over low heat; add wine. Add onion and cook for 15 minutes. Stir in mushrooms and cook for 10 minutes. Remove vegetables from skillet; keep warm. Season liver with salt and pepper. Saute for ½ minute on each side for rare doneness or 1 minute on each side for medium-well doneness. Place on warm platter and top with vegetables.

Venison heart may be prepared by the same method.

Yield: 4 servings

Charley Dickey
Tallahassee, Florida

"Providence gave me three sons, only about a year and a half apart; and since it was not possible for me to give them what we usually call the advantages of wealth, I made up my mind to do my best by them. I decided primarily to make them sportsmen, for I have a conviction that to be a sportsman is a mighty long step in the direction of being a man. I thought also that if a man brings up his sons to be hunters, they will never grow away from him. Rather the passing years will only bring them closer, with a thousand happy memories of the woods and fields. Again, a hunter never sits around home forlornly, not knowing what in the world to do with his leisure. His interest in nature will be such that he can delight in every season, and he has resources within himself that will make life always seem worth while."

Archibald Rutledge

Mexican Torte

1   (13½ ounce) package hot roll mix
1   pound ground venison
1   cup chopped onion
1   envelope taco seasoning
1   (10 ounce) package frozen chopped spinach
1   cup cottage cheese
    Salt and black pepper to taste
1   egg
1   teaspoon water

Prepare hot roll mix according to package directions; set dough aside. Saute ground venison and onion in skillet, stirring until well browned; drain excess grease. Add taco seasoning to meat. Cook spinach according to package directions; drain and press to remove excess moisture. Mix cottage cheese with spinach and season with salt and pepper. Divide roll dough into 3 portions; roll each into a circle to fit a springform pan. Grease bottom and sides of pan. Place 1 dough circle, add meat mixture, another dough circle, spinach-cheese mixture and last dough circle in pan. Let rise about 1 hour. Score top layer of dough with sharp knife, marking 6 sections. Brush with wash made from egg and water. Bake at 350 degrees for 45 to 50 minutes.

Yield: 3 or 4 servings

John and Denise Phillips
Fairfield, Alabama

Venison Sausage

4   pounds lean ground venison
1   pound ground pork fat
2   teaspoons salt
½   teaspoon black pepper
2   teaspoons ground sage
¼   teaspoon ground red pepper

Combine venison, fat and seasonings; mix well. Shape mixture into small patties. Fry in electric skillet at 350 degrees.

Yield: 10 to 12 servings

Lois Partridge
Tucker, Georgia

Westervelt Venison Loaf

10	pounds boned lean venison
1	pound beef kidney fat or beef tallow
1	pound mild pork sausage
	Seasoned salt
	Salt and black pepper
3	eggs, lightly beaten
2	cups milk
¼	cup chopped onion
½	green bell pepper, chopped
	Ketchup

Remove all fat from venison. Grind venison, kidney fat and sausage through a meat grinder. Season meat with salts and pepper. Put mixture through grinder twice. Combine eggs, milk, onion and green pepper; mix with meat until well blended. Shape mixture into oval loaves about 3 inches high. Place in greased 9x5x3-inch loafpans; spread top of each loaf with ketchup. Bake at 350 degrees for 2 to 2½ hours.

Loaf can be served as entree, may be rewarmed and is excellent for sandwiches. It may also be frozen.

Yield: 36 servings

Charley Dickey
Tallahassee, Florida

Waterfowl

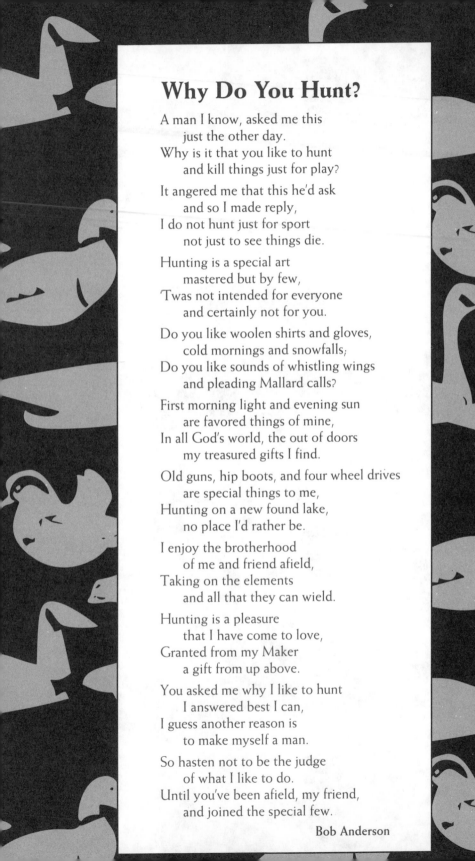

Why Do You Hunt?

A man I know, asked me this
    just the other day.
Why is it that you like to hunt
    and kill things just for play?

It angered me that this he'd ask
    and so I made reply,
I do not hunt just for sport
    not just to see things die.

Hunting is a special art
    mastered but by few,
'Twas not intended for everyone
    and certainly not for you.

Do you like woolen shirts and gloves,
    cold mornings and snowfalls;
Do you like sounds of whistling wings
    and pleading Mallard calls?

First morning light and evening sun
    are favored things of mine,
In all God's world, the out of doors
    my treasured gifts I find.

Old guns, hip boots, and four wheel drives
    are special things to me,
Hunting on a new found lake,
    no place I'd rather be.

I enjoy the brotherhood
    of me and friend afield,
Taking on the elements
    and all that they can wield.

Hunting is a pleasure
    that I have come to love,
Granted from my Maker
    a gift from up above.

You asked me why I like to hunt
    I answered best I can,
I guess another reason is
    to make myself a man.

So hasten not to be the judge
    of what I like to do.
Until you've been afield, my friend,
    and joined the special few.

Bob Anderson

The Spirit

There is a spirit in the Southern outdoors, a spirit more often than not defying description. It is a spirit of the same nature that almost certainly exists in the woods and waters of the Far North, the Midwest and other geographic locales as well. Wherever sportsmen venture forth, regional boundaries notwithstanding, there is a common bond, a tie that binds. But the Southern outdoor spirit is special, if only because it is ours.

Our Spirit is that of long-dead grandfathers and grandfathers yet living that compels us to carry on the outdoor sporting tradition in spite of those special interests that would willingly, and often enthusiastically, watch it fade into nothingness. It is a madly passionate love affair with the same wild creatures: the bluegills, the bass, the bobwhite quail and the whitetail deer our forebears avidly pursued and likewise cherished. It is The Spirit that motivates all true sportsmen, past and present, to stand up and speak out against the wanton destruction and abuse of our natural resources and heritage, even at the risk of damaged reputation and community standing.

The Spirit is there in a warm pipeful of Sir Walter Raleigh Aromatic lit with the red, glowing end of a campfire kindling strip on a crisp evening after a deer hunt. It is there in the circle of strangers gathered at the boat ramp, willingly sharing what little they know about a mutually unfamiliar body of water. The Spirit burns brightly, too, in the eyes of our sons and daughters when that first four-inch bream comes to hand or when the first gray squirrel succumbs to the sharp crack of a single-shot .22 amid the oaks and hickories of a hardwood river bottom forest.

If you seek The Spirit, look for it in the countenance of a special kind of hunter who has yet to score, with the end of deer season fast approaching. His material investment is a large one for a salaried man with a family to support. He owns a new bolt-action .30-06 for which he scrimped and saved for two years. He was, unbeknownst to his wife, forced to dip into the kids' savings account to purchase the quality scope he thought was needed. He is no Great White Hunter by anyone's standards but quite capable nonetheless. This season he has just been plain unlucky.

Today the same man sat in a tree stand for five solid hours only to let a rutting buck in pursuit of two sexy does outquick him and move swiftly out of range. He chuckles over the incident, still considering the day's outing a real, if minor, success. He has, in all his years of hunting, never before played eyewitness to the reckless abandon with which a monarch whitetail collects his harem. He has never heard the sex grunt of a buck deer in the throes of the rut. This day he has experienced both and reflects on the time as having been well spent. On the very real possibility of this particular season ending on a deerless note and his larder remaining empty of venison for another nine months, he comments, "There's always next year."

He has The Spirit.

We would be naive beyond description to think that The Spirit resides in us all. There are those Southern outdoorsmen who have never felt The Spirit nor been moved by it even once. Or maybe, just maybe, they have never taken the time to notice it. There will forever be those who cannot see the forest for the trees. For them, The Spirit will never encompass anything other than the catching of fish or the shooting of game. It is the way of things. The poor will always be among us.

But for those in whom The Spirit burns deeply, there is not time to dwell on such things. There are too many things to be savored between beginning and end to think too strongly about the game's conclusion. The Spirit, outcome notwithstanding, makes all endings somehow worthwhile.

If The Spirit is in us, we need never fear losing it. It never deserts us, never goes away. If you would have it as your own, do not search too hard or too long. Far better to allow it to find you.

And find you it will, in an Arkansas pin oak swamp, a Mississippi quail covert, a Carolina turkey blind or a north Georgia trout stream. In all those places is the Southern Outdoor Spirit. It is there, behind the limestone outcropping, in the boughs of the cypress tree, beneath the surface of the river slough where the water is deepest.

It is there. If you'll but see it.

Bob Kornegay
Blakely, Georgia
from *Buddies and Bobtales*

Duck in Orange Juice

1	duck
	Salt
	Chopped apples
	Chopped celery
	Chopped onion
4 or 5	slices bacon
1	cup orange juice

Season duck cavity with salt. Combine equal portions of coarsely chopped apples, celery and onion; spoon into duck cavity and stitch opening to secure stuffing. Saute bacon in large roaster or Dutch oven until nearly crisp; remove slices. Brown duck in bacon drippings. Add orange juice (add more juice if necessary to measure ½ inch deep in pan). Arrange bacon over duck. Simmer, covered, turning occasionally and basting with pan liquid. Cook large duck for 45 minutes to 1 hour; cook small duck for 30 minutes. To serve, remove duck from pan, slice meat and ladle pan liquid over slices.

Yield: 3 to 5 servings

Jim Dean
Division of Conservation Education
North Carolina Wildlife Resources Commission
Raleigh, North Carolina

Duck Breast a la Oscar

2 to 2½	pounds duck breast, cut in 1-inch strips
2	cups fine cracker crumbs
1	teaspoon salt
	Black pepper to taste
¾	cup butter

Place duck strips with crumbs, salt and pepper in plastic bag. Store in refrigerator overnight. To prepare, melt butter in skillet and heat until frothy. Place duck strips in skillet in single layer. Cook over low heat for 2 to 3 minutes or until blood rises to top of duck strips, turn, and cook on other side.

Yield: 6 to 8 servings

Steve Vaughn
Paducah, Kentucky

Barren River Duck Breast

½   cup milk
1   egg
1   cup all-purpose flour
1   tablespoon salt
1   tablespoon black pepper
     Breast fillets from 4 or 5 mallards, cut in 1-inch strips
1   cup vegetable oil

Combine milk and egg. Mix flour, salt and pepper. Dip duck strips in egg mixture and dredge in flour mixture. Fry in hot oil in large skillet over medium heat until brown. Serve as entree.

For a more traditional flavor, soak duck breasts in sweet milk overnight.

Yield: 3 or 4 servings

Howard P. Lindsey
Bowling Green, Kentucky

Baked Duck in a Bag

2   tablespoons all-purpose flour
1½   cups orange juice
2   ducks
½   cup melted butter or margarine
         Salt and black pepper to taste
2 or 3   apples, chopped
2   stalks celery, chopped
2   small oranges, sliced
         Red currant or wild plum jelly

Shake flour in large plastic roasting bag and place in 2-inch deep roasting pan. Add orange juice to flour and stir until thoroughly mixed. Wipe ducks with damp cloth. Brush outside and cavity of ducks with butter and sprinkle with salt and pepper. Spoon apple and celery into cavity of each duck. Place ducks in bag. Close with twist tie and cut 6 ½-inch slits in top of bag. Bake at 350 degrees for 1½ hours. Remove, slice and serve with garnish of orange slices topped with teaspon of jelly.

Yield: 6 servings

Pam Strickland
Natchez, Mississippi

Roast Duck with Wild Rice Stuffing

½   cup wild rice
1   small onion, minced
⅓   cup minced celery
⅓   cup chopped green bell pepper
1   tablespoon butter
2   tablespoons sauterne wine
½   teaspoon salt
1   duck, mallard preferred
     Salt and black pepper
     Garlic powder
     Melted butter
     Sauterne wine
     Poultry seasoning

Prepare rice according to package directions. Saute onion, celery and pepper in 1 tablespoon butter until tender; do not brown. Add vegetable mixture with 2 tablespoons wine and ½ teaspoon salt to cooked rice. Blot duck with paper towel to dry. Sprinkle with salt, pepper and a dash of garlic powder. Spoon rice mixture into duck cavity. Secure legs. Place in shallow baking pan. Bake at 450 degrees for 45 minutes to 1 hour, basting frequently with sauce made of melted butter, sauterne and poultry seasoning. If duck browns too rapidly, reduce oven temperature to 375 degrees and bake slightly longer. Large ducks should be baked at 350 degrees for 1½ hours or until well done.

Wild rice brings out the best flavor in duck. Use regular wild rice, not a white and wild rice mixture.

Yield: 2 servings

Sam Roberson
Lobelville, Tennessee

Bob's Duck Shish-Ka-Bobs

4	duck breast halves, skinned and boned
1	(16 ounce) can pineapple chunks
1	(8 ounce) bottle Italian dressing
12	cherry tomatoes
1	green bell pepper, cut into 12 squares
12	fresh mushrooms
1	(6 ounce) can orange juice concentrate
⅔	cup Worcestershire sauce

Slice duck breast halves into 3 lengthwise strips. Drain pineapple chunks, reserving juice. Combine juice and Italian dressing and use this to marinate meat for at least three hours. Alternate skewering pieces of meat, pineapple chunks, cherry tomatoes, bell pepper pieces, and mushrooms on shish-ka-bob skewers. Reserve marinade for basting sauce while cooking. Combine marinade, Worcestershire sauce, and orange juice concentrate in a saucepan and bring to a boil; reduce heat and let this basting sauce simmer five minutes. Grill kabobs over medium coals, turning frequently and brushing with sauce. 15 to 20 minutes is plenty of grilling time; do not overcook! Reheat any leftover sauce and pour over kabobs when serving.

Serves 6

Robert Hitt Neill
Brownspur, Mississippi

Broiled or Grilled Teal

This works equally as well with doves, snipe, woodcock, quail, grouse, and most other small game birds.

Breasted teal
Lemon-Pepper Marinade
Bacon slices

Sprinkle teal breasts all over with Lemon-Pepper Marinade, to suit your taste. Wrap each teal in a slice of bacon and anchor with a toothpick. Grill teal over medium coals, turning occasionally, for about 20 minutes, or until meat is done to your taste. On an open campfire, individual teal may be skewered on a hardwood stick and cooked as one would a hot dog.

Robert Hitt Neill
Brownspur, Mississippi

Duck Gumbo

1   cup all-purpose flour
½   cup vegetable oil
1   cup chopped celery
1   cup chopped onion
1   (10 ounce) can tomatoes with chilies
1   (16 ounce) can tomatoes, broken up
1   pound okra, sliced
1   gallon water
2   pounds cooked duck meat
½   cup chopped green onion
½   cup chopped green bell pepper
½   cup chopped parsley
     Garlic powder to taste
     Salt and black pepper to taste

Add flour to hot oil in heavy skillet; cook to form dark roux. Add celery and onion; cook for 30 minutes. Transfer mixture to large stockpot. Add tomatoes, okra and water; simmer for 1 hour. Stir in duck and remaining vegetables. Cook until meat is tender and gumbo is thickened. Season with parsley, garlic, salt and pepper.

Yield: 10 to 12 servings

Callie C. Spiller Jr.
Greensboro, North Carolina

"I have a philosophy which teaches me that certain game birds and animals are apparently made to be hunted, because of their peculiar food value and because their character lends zest to the pursuit of them. It has never seemed to me to be too far-fetched to suppose that Providence placed game here for a special purpose."
Archibald Rutledge

Kentucky Gumbo

Howard Lindsey recommends experimenting with this gumbo to "develop your own style...then the guys at the Deer Camp may never let you rotate off as 'Camp Cook.'"

4	duck breasts, boned and cut in chunks
3	chicken breasts, boned and cut in chunks
	Water
1	cup all-purpose flour
½	cup vegetable oil
1	pound kielbasa sausage, cut in chunks
1	large onion, diced
1	green bell pepper, diced
1	tablespoon minced garlic
1	pound frozen okra slices, thawed
1	(8 ounce) can tomato sauce
1	(6 ounce) can tomato paste
1	tablespoon hot pepper sauce
1½	teaspoons gumbo file
4	cups chicken broth
2	pounds uncooked Cajun seasoned or white rice

Cook duck and chicken in water to cover in large stockpot just until meat is cooked; do not overcook. Drain well. Add flour to hot oil in stockpot over medium heat; cook, stirring constantly, to form caramel-colored roux; do not burn. Add duck, chicken, sausage, vegetables, tomato sauce and paste and seasonings to roux. Cook, stirring frequently, for 8 to 9 minutes or until vegetables begin to soften. Reduce heat and add broth. Prepare rice according to package directions. Serve 1 cup cooked rice with 1 cup gumbo.

Yield: 12 servings

Howard P. Lindsey
Bowling Green, Kentucky

Duck Stew

The dark red meat of wild ducks has a flavor closer to beef or liver than fowl. Humberto Fontova recommends using beef recipes rather than those intended for fowl. This dish tastes like lean beef stew.

	Ducks, skin removed and quartered
	Bottled brown bouquet sauce
	Butter
	Potatoes, diced
	Celery, diced
	Carrots, diced
	Onion, diced
1	(15 ounce) can beef broth
½	cup cooking sherry
2	tablespoons steak sauce
	Milk
	Cornstarch
	Cooked rice

Season ducks by brushing with bouquet sauce. Brown in butter. Remove from skillet. Brown vegetables in butter. Combine ducks and vegetables in pressure saucepan or cooker. Add broth, sherry and steak sauce. Cook under pressure for 25 minutes. Thicken cooking liquid with small amount of milk mixed with cornstarch. Serve over rice.

Humberto Fontova
Covington, Louisiana

Kentucky Duck Salad

A favorite dish served at wild game dinners in the Lair of the Ancient Hunter (a Paducah gathering place for assorted outdoor types, rednecks, ne'erdowells, et al), this salad is easily prepared.

2	mallards or other puddle ducks
	Water
1	stalk celery, chopped
1	cup sweet pickle relish
1	dozen hard-cooked eggs, chopped
2	tablespoons lemon juice
1	cup mayonnaise
	Salt and black pepper to taste
	Pecans (optional)

Place ducks in large saucepan with water to cover. Simmer until very tender. Drain, remove skin, bone and chop coarsely. Combine chopped duck with celery, relish, eggs, lemon juice, mayonnaise, salt and pepper; mix thoroughly. Sprinkle with pecans. Chill for 2 hours or overnight.

Pheasant or rabbit may be substituted for ducks.

Yield: 10 to 12 servings

Uncle Russ Chittenden
Paducah, Kentucky

"I think the rod and gun better for boys than the saxophone and the fudge sundae. In the first place, there is something inherently manly and home-bred and truly American in that expression, "shooting straight." The hunter learns that reward comes from hard work; he learns from dealing with nature that a man must have a deep respect for the great natural laws."

Archibald Rutledge

Twice-Stuffed Goose

3	large onions, chopped
¼	cup butter
2	(4 ounce) cans chopped mushrooms, drained
2	cups pitted green olives
3	(7½ ounce) packages brown and long-grained rice mix
1	large goose
3	(10¾ ounce) cans cream of mushroom soup, undiluted
1	(2 ounce) jar diced pimiento

Saute onion in butter until tender. Add mushrooms, stirring gently. Add olives; mix and simmer; do not burn. Prepare rice according to package directions, cooking until almost all water is evaporated. Set aside to cool. Add onion mixture to rice and mix well. Spoon rice mixture into goose, filling cavity and placing remaining rice in and around the goose in the roasting pan. Bake, covered, at 350 degrees for 1 hour; reduce oven temperature to 300 degrees and bake several hours. Check for doneness; fork should easily pierce goose. Remove from oven. Scoop stuffing from bird cavity, then mix with stuffing outside goose and with pan liquids. Spoon as much of stuffing back into cavity as possible. Mix remainder with soup; mixture will be thick. Spoon a 1-inch layer of soup mixture over breast and upper side of goose. Bake, uncovered, until goose is very tender. Sprinkle pimiento on top of goose for flavor and garnish.

Yield: 6 to 8 servings

John and Denise Phillips
Fairfield, Alabama

Fried Goose Breast Fillets

2   Canada goose breast fillets
    Italian salad dressing
    All-purpose flour
    Vegetable oil

Cut fillets across the grain into ½-inch slices, then cut into 1-inch lengths. Marinate in dressing for 3 to 4 hours or overnight. Drain. Dredge pieces in flour and fry in hot oil for 3 to 4 minutes on each side. Drain on paper towels. Serve on wooden picks.

Yield: 16 to 20 servings

Larry Berry
Paducah, Kentucky

Specklebelly Goose

1   goose
    Creole seasoning
    Olive oil
1   tablespoon chopped garlic
1   onion, chopped
1   green bell pepper, chopped
1   pound link sausage, sliced

Season goose with Creole seasoning and brown in olive oil in Dutch oven on stove top. After goose is browned, pour off excess grease only. Turn goose belly down and add remaining ingredients. Add enough water to cover half the bird and bake, covered, in 300 degree oven for 3 hours.

Terry P. Shaughnessy
Hackberry, Louisiana

Upland Birds

Some hae meat, wha canna eat;
Some wad eat, but hae no meat;
But we hae meat, an' we can eat;
So let the Lord be thankit!

Robert Burns

Gobbler

Your glottal thunder
    Echoes of eternity
        In the fog-clad river bottom,

And the first glint of morning sunlight
    shatters the prism of
        iridescent feathers.

While nuances of Nineveh
    are printed in cuneiform
        with the passage of your track.

Billy Ellis
from Hunter to the Dawn

Under a bright and starry sky,
Dig the grave and let me lie.
Glad did I live, and gladly die,
And I lay me down with a will.

And this be the verse that ye 'grave for me:
Here he lies where he longed to be;
Home is the sailor, home from the sea,
And the hunter, home from the hill.

Robert Louis Stevenson

The Elixir of Life

I've always heard the old saying, "What goes around, comes around". And I've seen it happen time and time again. I thought about it the other morning, when my son got up before I did for a turkey hunt. My alarm had not yet gone off when I sniffed a wonderful odor from the kitchen. The boy was making coffee for his old daddy!

I had been just about his age when my old daddy had taught me to make coffee, ostensibly so I could bring him a cup in bed on hunting camp. I was now realizing that it was not so much the hot cup in bed that Big Robert desired so much as the SMELL of the black brew to wake up to!

I am aware that modern technology has provided us with timers on modern coffee makers so that one can build his coffee the night before to wake up to the next morning. However, I am partial to boiled coffee: the REAL stuff, with grounds in the bottom of the pot, some of which pour into your cup so that you dare not drink the final swallow. Coffee that you dare not leave a spoon in too long. Coffee that has enough "sumption" to hold its heat like a brick from the hearth. Coffee that's good to the last bite!

Boiled coffee, my mother-in-law Miss Mabel used to say, should only be stirred with a green stick. You boil the water in a kettle, pour it over the grounds in the coffeepot (one scoop for each two cups is my prescription), let it boil up, remove the pot and stir it down, set it back on the fire, do that three times, then run a cup of cold water down the spout to settle the grounds. Most of the grounds. Some pour out into each cup and that's all right; it's kind of like ashes on a hot dog, part of the Southern Outdoor Culture.

There was a ritual involved when Big Robert sat me down to explain coffee making that day; it was almost like an old Indian medicine man passing down his secrets to his son. I was a junior in high school when he spoke man-to-man to me: "Son, I've carried you for sixteen years. Now it's time for you to carry me. But I ain't over the hill yet. If I feel like totin' somethin', I want you to let me; if I don't feel like it, you tote it. But there are two things you get to do all the time now: you get to scull the boat while we're fishin' and you get to make coffee in the mornings at camp and bring me a cup in bed!"

"But, Daddy, I don't even drink coffee," I protested.

"I'm gonna drink it. You're gonna make it. And I'm fixin' to teach you how."

That was the beginning of my love affair with strong, black, boiled coffee. To heck with this new-fangled communistic decaffeinated stuff! And they threw the tea overboard, remember?

Coffee BELONGS to be invigorating, to have a kick to it. That rich, brownish, slightly tangy, faintly earthy smell that neither rises nor falls but hovers at shoulder level throughout the house, gives us a reason to start the day. Even if today happens to be the day they're foreclosing on your family farm or the day you're scheduled for hemorrhoid surgery, for just a little while you can experience the sheer pleasure of hovering over that first cup of black brew. I love the smell of caffeine in the morning!

In his book *Dealers Choice,* Alabamian Tom Kelly declares that the Confederate Army performed the greatest feat known to military history by surviving four years of war on a brew of ground roast acorns as a substitute for coffee. No doubt that stuff was also decaffeinated. Heck, I don't give a flip about hunting, fishing or anything else for that matter, without my morning coffee. I shudder to even think about having to get up and shoot Yankees after a cup of acorn juice!

Have you ever considered that the Dark Ages ended and the Renaissance began when Christopher Columbus discovered the Americas—and coffee?

Robert Hitt Neill
Brownspur, Mississippi
from *Don't Fish Under the Dingleberry Tree*

Delicious Dove Casserole

12	doves
1	(10½ ounce) can chicken broth
6	tablespoons butter, divided
2½	tablespoons all-purpose flour
⅔	cup half and half
⅔	cup breadcrumbs
⅔	cup chopped green bell pepper
⅔	cup chopped onion
2	tablespoons chopped parsley
½	teaspoon ground sage
½	teaspoon salt
	Freshly ground black pepper to taste
¼	cup sherry

Cook whole doves in broth until tender. Remove breasts and dice meat. Reserve 4 cups. Blend 3 tablespoons butter with flour and half and half. Saute breadcrumbs, vegetables, parsley and sage in 3 tablespoons butter. Combine breadcrumb mixture, thickened cream and dove meat in skillet. Season with salt and pepper, add sherry and simmer for 25 to 30 minutes. Transfer to casserole and broil for a few minutes.

If additional moisture is needed while sauteeing vegetables with breadcrumbs, add dove cooking liquid.

Yield: 4 servings

Jim Dean
Division of Conservation Education
North Carolina Wildlife Resources Commission
Raleigh, North Carolina

Betsy's Sherried Doves

Betsy cooks this dove recipe in a cast-iron skillet. A new skillet can be seasoned by rubbing vegetable oil in it and then placing it in a hot oven until it smokes.

12	dove breasts
¼	teaspoon salt
¼	teaspoon pepper
¼	cup butter or margarine
2	cups sherry
2	tablespoons cornstarch
¼	cup water
	Hot cooked rice

Sprinkle doves with salt and pepper. Melt butter in a 10-inch cast-iron skillet. Place doves breast-up in skillet and pour in sherry. Cover and bake at 400 degrees for 35 to 40 minutes. Remove doves and keep warm; reserve 2 cups pan drippings (add water to measure 2 cups, if necessary). Combine cornstarch and ¼ cup water, stirring well, then stir into pan drippings. Bring this mixture to a boil over medium heat; boil for 1 minute. Serve this gravy and doves over rice.

Serves 3 couples.

Snipe and woodcock may be substituted for doves, if desired.

Betsy Neill
Brownspur, Mississippi

"Hunting is not incompatible with the deepest and most genuine love of nature....It has always seemed to me that any man is a better man for being a hunter. This sport confers a certain constant alertness, and develops a certain ruggedness of character that, in these days of too much civilization, is refreshing; moreover, it allies us to the pioneer past. In a deep sense, this great land of ours was won for us by hunters."

Archibald Rutledge

Grouse au Vin

2	grouse, quartered
1	large sweet onion, sliced
1	bay leaf
6	whole cloves
3 or 4	dried sage leaves
1	(32 ounce) bottle port wine
2	cups all-purpose flour
1½	teaspoons salt
1	teaspoon black pepper
½	cup butter

Combine grouse, onion, herbs and wine; marinate for 2 days in the refrigerator. Drain meat, reserving liquid, and blot with paper towel to dry. Combine flour, salt and pepper. Dredge meat in seasoned flour and saute in butter. Place meat in casserole and pour reserved marinade over meat. Bake, covered, at 300 degrees for 1½ hours or until tender.

Yield: 4 servings

Kay L. Richey
Buckley, Michigan

Grouse in Mushroom Gravy

2	grouse, cut in serving-sized pieces
2	(10¾ ounce) cans cream of mushroom soup, undiluted
¼	cup minced celery
¼	cup minced green bell pepper
¼	cup minced onion

Place grouse pieces in casserole. Spoon soup over meat. Stir in vegetables. Bake, tightly covered, at 350 degrees for 45 minutes to 1 hour.

Snowshoe hare, vension and other dark meat small game may be substituted for grouse.

Yield: 6 servings

Sam Roberson
Lobelville, Tennessee

Grouse au Gratin

2   slices bacon
4   grouse breasts
     Seasoned flour
2   (10¾ ounce) cans Cheddar cheese soup,
     undiluted
1   soup can milk

Fry bacon until crisp; drain and crumble. Dredge breasts in flour and saute in bacon drippings. Place in casserole. Combine soup and milk; pour over breasts. Sprinkle with crumbled bacon. Bake, covered, at 325 degrees for 1½ hours.

Yield: 2 servings

Dave Richey
Buckley, Michigan

"Again, there is a comradeship among hunters that has always seemed to me one of the finest human relationships. When fellow sportsmen meet in the woods or fields or the lonely marshes, they meet as friends who understand each other. There is a fine democracy about all this that is a mighty wholesome thing for young people to know. As much as I do anything else in life I treasure my comradeships with old, grizzled woodsmen. Hunting alone could have made us friends."

Archibald Rutledge

Hawaiian Pheasant

2   pheasants, cut in serving-sized pieces
¼   cup soy sauce
1   teaspoon ginger
½   teaspoon salt
1   tablespoon dried minced onion
½   cup orange juice
1   (16 ounce) can pineapple chunks, drained and juice reserved
2   teaspoons cornstarch
¼   cup cold water

Place pheasant pieces in slow-cooker. Combine soy sauce, ginger, salt, onion, orange and pineapple juice; pour over pheasant. Cook, covered, on low setting for 6 to 8 hours. Remove pheasant pieces and set aside. Mix cornstarch with water; gradually add to hot liquid in cooker and heat until thickened. Add pineapple chunks and pheasant pieces; heat thoroughly.

Yield: 6 servings

Joan Cone
Williamsburg, Virginia

All-Day Pheasant

1   pheasant, cut in serving-sized pieces
    Butter
    Onions, quartered
    Celery, cut in chunks
    Carrots, cut in chunks
    Potatoes, peeled and quartered
½   (10¾ ounce) can cream of mushroom soup, undiluted
½   (10¾ ounce) can cream of celery soup, undiluted

Brown pheasant pieces in butter; place in slow cooker. Add vegetables to pheasant. Pour soup over vegetables. Cook, covered, at low setting for about 6½ hours or until pheasant is tender and vegetables are soft.

Yield: 3 or 4 servings

John and Denise Phillips
Fairfield, Alabama

Quail in a Bag

1	tablespoon all-purpose flour
½	cup white wine
½	teaspoon brown bouquet sauce
2	stalks celery, coarsely chopped
1	(2 ounce) can sliced mushrooms, undrained
6	quail, split in halves
	Melted butter or margarine
	Salt to taste

Place flour in 10x16-inch plastic roasting bag; place bag in 2-inch deep roasting pan. Combine wine and bouquet sauce; pour into bag and mix well with flour. Add celery and mushrooms with liquid to bag. Brush quail halves with butter and season with salt. Place quail on vegetables in bag. Close with twist tie and cut 6½-inch slits in top of bag. Bake at 350 degrees for 1 hour. To serve, spoon bag gravy over quail.

Yield: 3 servings

Joan Cone
Williamsburg, Virginia

Wild Turkey

Wild turkeys were nearly extinct in many parts of North America for many years. Their passing brought a few tears to the eyes of American hunters. Fortunately, about 40 years ago wildlife biologists implemented a program that restored this largest game bird to huntable numbers. Turkey hunting is popular because in many states it is legal during the spring months when other seasons are closed. Some states have a fall season too. Hunting these birds can be frustrating. They have eyesight comparable to an eagle, can hear very well and are skittish. One false move, a glimpse of a hunter's skin and they are long gone. But when the hunter does everything right and the turkey does something wrong, the result is a gobbler than can weigh 20 pounds. Dressed out, that bird will yield about 15 pounds of meat, enough for a beautiful Thanksgiving dinner.

Turkeys are not as dry as many game birds. A dressing will add some moisture during cooking.

Fried Turkey with Running Gear Gravy

1	(15 pound) turkey
	Cold water
	All-purpose flour
2	cups milk
3	eggs, beaten
2	cups breadcrumbs
	Vegetable oil

Skin, rather than pluck, the turkey. Fillet the breast meat and re-move the heavy breast tendon; cut breast steaks across the grain in ½-inch thick slices and several inches long. Soak in cold water for 3 hours to remove excess blood. Cut apart legs, thighs, wings, neck and back. Cook dark meat in water until it separates from bones. Chop meat, season to taste and add to cooking liquid. Thicken with flour just before serving. Mix milk and eggs in bowl. Dip breast fillets in egg mixture, breadcrumbs, egg and breadcrumbs. Deep fry in oil at 365 degrees, cooking for 7 to 10 minutes or until golden brown.

Pour gravy over breast fillets as well as potatoes or rice.

Yield: 8 servings

Rob Keck
Edgefield, South Carolina

Keck's Smoked Wild Turkey

1	(12 to 14 pound) turkey, dressed weight and skin intact
1	teaspoon salt
1	tablespoon black pepper
1	teaspoon sage
½	cup melted butter or margarine
1	clove garlic
1	large onion, quartered
½	cup sauterne

Soak turkey in cold water for 3 hours to remove excess blood. Rub turkey with salt, pepper, sage and margarine. Place garlic and onions inside breast and splash cavity with sauterne. Place on water smoker rack. Add pecan or hickory chips to coals. Cook, covered, until coals die, usually 10 to 12 hours. To hasten smoking, bake bird in oven at 350 degrees for 2 hours, then place in water smoker.

Yield: 6 to 8 servings

Rob Keck
Edgefield, South Carolina

Hot Turkey Casserole

2	cups chopped cooked turkey
½	cup chopped almonds
2	cups chopped celery
⅓	cup chopped green bell pepper
2	tablespoons chopped pimiento
1	cup (4 ounces) shredded Swiss or Cheddar cheese
½	cup mayonnaise
2	tablespoons lemon juice
1	teaspoon salt
¼	teaspoon black pepper
1	cup crushed potato chips

Combine turkey, almonds, vegetables, cheese, mayonnaise, lemon juice and seasonings. Pour mixture into greased 2-quart casserole. Bake at 350 degrees for 30 minutes. Sprinkle potato chips on top of turkey mixture and bake until chips are lightly browned.

Yield: 4 to 6 servings

John and Denise Phillips
Fairfield, Alabama

Smoked Wild Turkey

1 to 2	cups cooking sherry
2	lemons, sliced
1	(10 to 20 pound) turkey
	Seasoned salt
	Thyme
	Poultry seasoning
	Melted butter

In electric smoker, place soaked hickory chips in appropriate place, partially fill the water pan and add sherry and lemons to water. In charcoal smoker, place charcoal in appropriate place, light and wait until flaming subsides. Place hickory chips on charcoal and place partially filled water pan above, adding sherry and lemons to water. Generously sprinkle turkey with seasoned salt, then add thyme and poultry seasoning to taste. If available, use a large syringe to inject melted butter and additional seasonings into carcass for flavor and extra moisture. Place turkey on rack and seal the smoker. For 8 to 12 pound turkey, use 10 pounds charcoal, 6 quarts water and allow 8 to 10 hours smoking time. For 13 to 16 pound turkey, use 12 pounds charcoal, 7 quarts water and allow 10 to 12 hours smoking time, and for 17 to 20 pound turkey, use 15 pounds charcoal, 8 quarts water and allow 12 to 14 hours smoking time.

Yield: 10 to 12 servings

John and Denise Phillips
Fairfield, Alabama

"...I want my boys to go through life making these humble contacts and learning from fellow human beings, many of them very unpretentious and simple-hearted, some of the ancient lore of nature that is one of the very finest heritages of our race. Nature always solves her own problems; and we can go far toward solving our own if we will listen to her teachings and consort with those who love her."

Archibald Rutledge

Roast Turkey with Magic Basting Pot Sauce

1	(8 ounce) can tomato sauce
6	cups water
4	stalks celery, cut in 3-inch pieces
1	large onion, peeled
	Turkey gizzard, neck and heart
1	teaspoon salt
½	teaspoon black pepper
	Whole Wheat Bread Stuffing
	Turkey
	Melted butter

Combine tomato sauce, water, vegetables, turkey parts and seasonings in 4-quart saucepan. Bring to a boil, then simmer during entire turkey roasting time. If liquid diminishes to less than half the original amount, add water. Prepare stuffing. Spoon into turkey cavity; do not pack. Secure legs and close opening to cavity. Rub turkey with butter and place, breast side up, in roasting pan. Cover with cheesecloth soaked in butter. Bake at 350 degrees. Ladle liquid from the simmering basting pot and pour over cheesecloth every 30 minutes. At halfway point of roasting time, turn turkey breast side down and pour pan drippings into basting pot. Continue basting. Turn turkey breast side up and remove cheesecloth 30 minutes before end of roasting time. For turkeys up to 6 pounds, roast for 20 to 25 minutes per pound; 7 to 16 pound turkeys, roast 15 to 20 minutes per pound, and 16 pound and larger turkeys, roast for 13 to 15 minutes per pound; add 3 minutes extra per pound for stuffed turkey. Place roasted turkey, breast side down, on platter and let stand for 20 minutes. Turn, slice and serve. Pour roasting pan liquid into basting pot. Strain and skim to remove excess fat. Mince gizzard and heart and add to mixture. Cook until thickened and serve gravy.

National Wild Turkey Federation, Inc.

Whole Wheat Bread Stuffing

1	pound chestnuts
	Boiling water
2	large onions, diced
4	stalks celery, cut in 1-inch pieces
3	tablespoons vegetable oil
1	pound fresh mushrooms, sliced
1	(16 ounce) loaf 100% whole wheat bread, toasted and torn or cubed
2	eggs, lightly beaten
¾	teaspoon salt
½	teaspoon black pepper
1	cup boiling water

Using a sharp knife, cut a cross on each chestnut. Boil in water for about 10 minutes or until shell opens, cool in cold water, peel and slice or dice; set aside. Saute onions and celery in oil in large saucepan until vegetables are tender and translucent. Add mushrooms and cook additional 10 minutes. Combine bread, chestnuts, vegetable mixture, eggs, seasonings and boiling water, mixing lightly but thoroughly. Spoon stuffing into bird but do not pack.

National Wild Turkey Federation, Inc.

Wild Turkey and Wild Rice

2   (10¾ ounce) cans cream of celery soup, undiluted
2   (10¾ ounce) cans cream of chicken soup, undiluted
2   soup cans water
1   envelope dry onion soup mix
1   pint mushrooms, sliced, or 1 (8 ounce) can mushrooms, drained
1   cup wild rice, soaked in hot water
1   cup uncooked white rice
¾   cup slivered almonds
18   pieces (½-inch thick and size of jumbo oyster) uncooked turkey
    Salt

Combine soup, water, soup mix, mushrooms, rice and almonds; spread evenly in 9x12x2-inch baking pan or casserole. Place turkey on top of soup mixture. Season turkey with salt. Bake, covered, at 350 degrees for 1 hour; remove cover and bake for 30 minutes or until rice is cooked.

Yield: 6 servings

Rob Keck
Edgefield, South Carolina

Old Poacher Fillet of Wild Turkey

1   turkey breast, skin removed
    Buttermilk
    All-purpose flour
    Salt and black pepper
    Vegetable oil

Using sharp boning knife, remove breast fillets from turkey. Cut fillets across grain in ⅜-inch thick slices; cut again into 2-inch pieces. Marinate pieces in buttermilk for 2 to 3 hours. Combine flour, salt and pepper. Drain turkey pieces, dredge in seasoned flour and fry in ½-inch depth of oil for 3 to 4 minutes per side or browned, turning once. Drain on paper towels.

Steve Fugate
Paducah, Kentucky

Braised Turkey

1	turkey
	Salt and black pepper to taste
1	pound salt pork, sliced
4	cups consomme
1	carrot sliced
1	onion, sliced
1	large stalk celery, chopped
1	bay leaf
2 or 3	parsley sprigs
	Pinch of thyme

Season turkey cavity with salt and pepper. Place in deep roasting pan. Stuff one-half of salt pork in cavity; use remainder to cover turkey, securing with wooden picks if necessary. Bake at 400 degrees for 1 hour. Combine consomme, vegetables and seasonings. Remove and discard salt pork. Add consomme mixture to turkey. Bake, tightly covered, at 300 degrees for 2 to 3 hours or until tender, basting frequently with pan liquids.

Yield: 10 to 12 servings

John and Denise Phillips
Fairfield, Alabama

Wild Turkey Breast Fillets with Milk Gravy

1	turkey breast, skin removed
	Vegetable oil
2	tablespoons all-purpose flour
	Milk
	Salt and black pepper to taste
	Chopped onion (optional)
	Chopped green bell pepper (optional)

Using sharp boning knife, remove breast fillets from turkey. Cut fillets across the grain into thin slices. Fry fillets in oil in skillet for 2 to 3 minutes on each side, turning once. Remove from skillet and cover to keep warm. Add flour to pan drippings. Add milk to about ½ depth of skillet, stirring well to smooth flour. Continue stirring until gravy thickens. Season with salt and pepper. Add onion or green pepper. Serve over hot biscuits with fillets.

Method and gravy works well on wild goose, venison backstrap or any bird with enough breast portion to fillet.

Sam H. Roberson
Lobelville, Tennessee

Wild Turkey Chili

2½	pounds boned turkey, cubed
1	cup chopped onion
½	cup chopped green bell pepper
	Vegetable oil
1	tablespoon salt
1	tablespoon chili powder
1½	teaspoons garlic powder
2	cups water
½	cup Wild Turkey bourbon
4	cups tomato puree
2	pounds kidney beans, cooked and drained
1	(16 ounce) package Monterey Jack cheese, coarsely grated

Saute turkey cubes, onion and green pepper in oil for 5 to 6 minutes or until turkey is no longer pink and onions are transluscent. Stir in seasonings. Transfer turkey mixture to stockpot. Add water, bourbon, tomato puree and beans. Simmer, covered, for 1 hour or longer. Serve each bowl with grated cheese.

Spicy and faintly sweet, turkey chili is great for those wishing to avoid red meats. Bourbon may be drunk, added to chili or both.

Yield: 10 to 12 servings

Howard P. Lindsey
Bowling Green, Kentucky

Wild Turkey Soup

1	turkey carcass
4 to 5	quarts water
4	medium carrots
1	small head cabbage
3	stalks celery
1	teaspoon salt
½	teaspoon black pepper
½	teaspoon poultry seasoning
	Leftover turkey gravy and stuffing
1	(16 ounce) package elbow macaroni, cooked

Remove meat from turkey carcass; set aside. Place carcass and water in large stockpot. Simmer for 2 hours or until meat separates from bones but not long enough for bones to fall apart. While carcass simmers, grind vegetables in a meat grinder, catching juices. Remove carcass from broth. Add vegetables, juices, seasonings, gravy and stuffing to broth; simmer for about 2 hours. Clean remaining meat from the bones and add all meat to soup. When vegetables are tender, add macaroni. Let stand several hours before serving to allow flavor to develop.

Yield: 8 to 10 servings

Rob Keck
Edgefield, South Carolina

"Yes, I have brought up my three boys to be hunters; and I know full well that when the wild creatures need no longer have any apprehensions about me, my grandchildren will be hard on their trail, pursuing with keen enjoyment and wholesome passion the sport of kings. While other boys are whirling in the latest jazz or telling dubious stories on street corners, I'd like to think that mine are deep in the lonely woods, far in the silent hills, listening to another kind of music, learning a different kind of lore."

Archibald Rutledge

Turkey Frittata

½	cup minced onion
1	tablespoon butter
8	eggs, separated
½	cup milk
1	teaspoon salt
1	teaspoon Worcestershire sauce
4 or 5	drops hot pepper sauce
2	cups cooked rice
1	(4 ounce) can chopped green chilies, undrained
1	medium tomato, chopped
2	cups chopped cooked turkey
½	cup (2 ounces) shredded Cheddar cheese

Saute onion in butter in 10-inch skillet over medium heat until onion is tender. Beat egg whites until fluffy but not dry; set aside. Beat egg yolks with milk and seasonings. Stir rice, chilies, tomatoes and turkey into milk mixture. Add egg whites. Pour mixture into skillet. Cook, covered, over medium low heat for 12 to 15 minutes or until surface is nearly firm. Sprinkle with cheese, cover, remove from heat and let stand for 10 minutes. If preferred, mixture may be poured into baking pan and baked at 350 degrees for 30 minutes.

Yield: 4 to 6 servings

John and Denise Phillips
Fairfield, Alabama

Turkey Macaroni Casserole

½	(8 ounce) package shell or elbow macaroni
½	cup butter
¼	cup unbleached flour
3	tablespoons nonfat dry milk powder
1	cup water
1	teaspoon salt
¼	teaspoon black pepper
1	(10¾ ounce) can golden mushroom soup, undiluted
1	cup frozen English peas, cooked
1½	cups chopped cooked turkey
¾	cup (3 ounces) shredded Cheddar cheese
½	cup breadcrumbs
1	tablespoon melted butter

Prepare macaroni according to package directions, drain and set aside. Melt ½ cup butter in large saucepan over low heat. Add flour and milk powder; cook for 1 minute, stirring constantly until smooth. Gradually add water and cook over medium heat, stirring constantly, until mixture is thickened. Add salt, pepper and soup; cook until bubbly, stirring frequently. Add macaroni, peas and turkey to sauce. Pour into lightly grease 1½-quart casserole. Sprinkle cheese over mixture and top with breadcrumbs mixed with melted butter. Bake at 350 degrees for 25 to 30 minutes.

Yleld: 4 servings

Pam Strickland
Natchez, Mississippi

Turkey Spaghetti Casserole

1	(8 ounce) package spaghetti
1	cup chopped celery
¼	cup chopped onion
3	tablespoons chopped green bell pepper
3	tablespoons butter
1½	cups turkey gravy
1	cup chicken broth
½	cup half and half
1	teaspoon salt
	Dash of pepper
1½	cups chopped cooked turkey
½	cup buttered soft breadcrumbs

Prepare spaghetti according to package directions, drain and set aside. Saute celery, onion and green pepper in butter. Add gravy, broth, cream, seasonings and turkey. Combine spaghetti and turkey sauce. Pour mixture into 2-quart casserole. Sprinkle top with crumbs. Bake at 350 degrees for 30 minutes.

Yield: 4 to 6 servings

John and Denise Phillips
Fairfield, Alabama

"When a father can see his boy follow and fairly kill our most wary and splendid game bird, I think the Old Man has a right to feel that his son's education is one to be proud of. I'd far rather have a son of mine able to climb a mountain and outwit the wary creatures of the wilderness than be able to dance the Brazilian busybody or be able to decide whether a lavender tie will match mauve socks. These little lisping men, these modern ruins, these lazy effeminates who could not tell you the difference between a bull and a bullet — it is not in these that the hope of America, that the hope of humanity, lies."

Archibald Rutledge

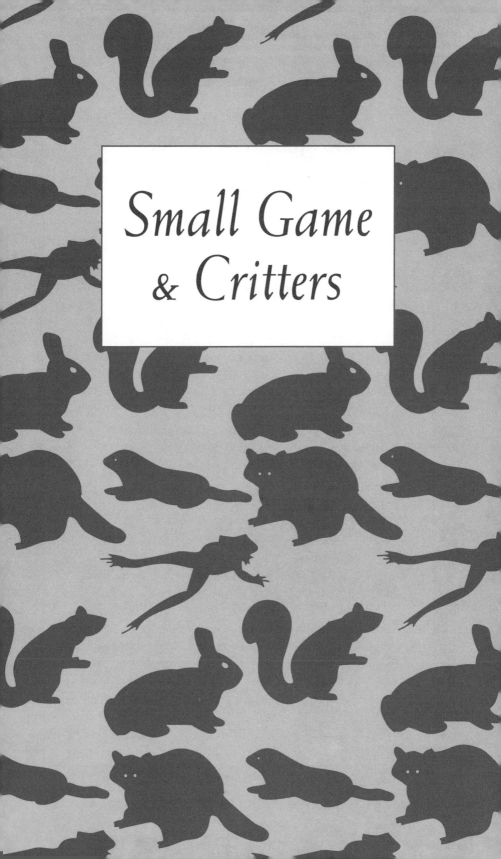

Small Game & Critters

The Sporting Calendar

from
The Ruination of Dude McElwee
*(upon the occasion of said Dude being elected to his
church's pulpit search committee during turkey season)*

Oh, Admiral Drake, your wisdom and smarts
    Are greater than Solomon's, you've won our hearts!
So now we come asking your wisest decree,
    For setting the seasons for Neill-McElwee.

Now, Admiral Drake, by anyone's reason,
    April's for one thing—that's turkey season.
By the same token (if Dude can remember)
    We always hunt deer in November, December.

The fishing is best in June and July
    (We still go in August but I don't know why!)
September's for dove, January's for duck,
    February's when we try our quail luck.

March is the month when we pack up our gear,
    Like decoys for ducks and rifles for deer;
Out comes the green camo, the mosquito gunk,
    For in April—remember?—we've turkeys to hunt.

In October, we're stiff, like a shirt full of starch,
    And we get out the gear that we packed up in March,
We reload our shells, plan places to hunt,
    While watching to see which team has to punt.

So Admiral Drake, we've asked for a ruling:
    To set preacher season and stop all this fooling.
The only month left is the merry one, May;
    That's when we'll hunt preachers, if we have our say!

Robert Hitt Neill
from *The Flaming Turkey*

Floating Florida Swamp Rabbits

Surviving in the marshy lowlands of central Florida despite man's intrusion in their habitat, the unique swamp rabbit once provided protein dinners for families living near the lakes and streams. Ironically, when civilization forced them to exodus their conventional territory, some survived on floating deserted islands where few hunters guessed their presence.

Floating islands in some of the larger lakes are as large as forty acres. Heavily weeded areas accumulated soil, then bushes, and later even trees thirty feet tall. The densely covered islands drifted at the whim of winds and currents, sometimes lodging on shorelines or even blocking boat trails leading to fish camps. Operators solicited helpers, attached lines to the island trees and with outboard motors at full throttle, towed the obstructions to obscure corners of the lake.

A story is told of a more than somewhat intoxicated fisherman on the lake one day when unseen boats were attached to the far side of the island, pulling the forty-acre mass through the open water. The drunk hurried back to camp and headed for home, declaring, "Gotta get to a doctor; I'm seeing things! Even the land is moving!"

Man and his unpenned dogs harassed the rabbits in the nearby marshes and by instinct the swamp rabbits fled, some taking up residence on these floating islands. It mattered not to them that their homeland moved back and forth across the lake; there was plenty of food and life on a manless island was easy. There was ample habitat for nesting, also.

Rabbits reproduce like...well, rabbits! A single healthy pair left unmolested and with plenty of food can have as many as thirty to fifty offspring in a single warm Florida year. In time, the floating islands became rabbit-producing incubators. The vegetation was thick but the hordes of rabbits literally began to eat themselves out of house and home!

Yet as the undergrowth was reduced, fishermen discovered the swamp bunnies and soon the word got around. Before a natural die-off occurred from overpopulation, hunters arrived with their beagles to harvest the extras and restore the balance of nature. Swamp rabbits became a delicacy for many Floridians, including Pulitzer Prize winner Marjorie Kinnan Rawlings who liked to hunt but "couldn't hit the broadside of a barn," according to her husband.

Swamp rabbits are a darker color than the more popular cottontail and about a third larger (as well as smarter, many veteran rabbit hunters believe). They are found around water and do not hesitate to use this natural obstacle to confuse hunting dogs and escape. Often they will criss-cross branches and creeks repeatedly until the beagles give up the chase. Cottontails when trailed will often circle and return to a few yards of the spot where they were jumped, but not swamp rabbits. They seem to rejoice in tricking pursuers by backtracking and losing even dogs with the best of noses. They have been seen to swim downstream for hundreds of feet, then emerge on the same side they left from and hightail it. They outfox the dogs.

One hunter recalls a day when he watched a swamp rabbit approach a stream with the trailing dogs barking in the distance. The rabbit ran across a leaning tree that spanned the stream and jumped to the ground to run a ways on the other side. Moments later, it returned to the tree, leaped back on it, ran to a point midstream and then jumped to a grassy tussock the size of a bathtub two feet below. It quickly nosed out a nest in the grass and buried itself there. Soon the dogs reached the tree, discovered that their quarry had crossed on it and the whole pack carefully maneuvered over the stream on the tree. Hitting the ground on the other side, they lost the track almost immediately. The hunter was so impressed that he just grinned and called off the dogs. The swamper deserved to survive that day, and did!

Little has been done by wildlife agencies to preserve or enhance the rabbit population though chemicals, land-clearing and encroaching civilization have taken their toll. But the uncanny fortitude and instincts of the swamp rabbit will keep it around for future generations, particularly in central Florida where the floating islands provide a haven for these grizzled, rough-looking creatures with white tail and long ears that have outfoxed so many packs of beagles for generations.

The swamp rabbit is a survivor!

W. Horace Carter
Hawthorne, Florida

No Peek Rabbit

1   rabbit, cut in serving-sized pieces
     Salt and black pepper to taste
1   cup smoke-flavored barbecue sauce

Season rabbit pieces with salt and pepper. Place in a slow-cooker and pour a small amount of barbecue sauce on each piece. Do not add water. Cook, covered, at low setting for 8 to 10 hours.

Yield: 2 servings

Elise Vachon
Marietta, Georgia

Rabbit Shish-Ka-Bobs

    Loins and hindquarters of 3 rabbits, boned and chunked
⅔   cup Worcestershire sauce
1   (8 ounce) bottle Italian Dressing
1   (8 ounce) jar mint jelly
12 cherry tomatoes
12 mushrooms
1   bell pepper, sliced into 12 pieces

Marinate the meat chunks for at least three hours in Italian Dressing. Alternate meat, cherry tomatoes, bell pepper slices, and mushrooms on shish-ka-bob skewers. Combine Italian Dressing marinade, Worcestershire sauce, and mint jelly in a saucepan and heat until it simmers for 5 minutes. Use this as a baste sauce. Grill shish-ka-bobs over medium coals for about 20 minutes, or until done to your taste, turning and basting frequently. Reheat remaining sauce to pour over shish-ka-bobs upon serving.

Yield: serves 6 couples, if the rabbits were good-sized

Robert Hitt Neill
Brownspur, Mississippi

Kentucky Burgoo

There are some "polite" burgoo recipes, says Tom Pearce, "but this one is from the back country folks that like to eat what they catch." He warns that this recipe, a combination of several versions of the same process, is not for the faint of heart. "The pile of bones beside the cauldron is enough to send some folks scurrying for the peanut butter and white bread," he reports. Burgoo, rich and meaty, tastes like a tangy stew with corn and other vegetables adding color and flavor. It can be eaten like a stew or served barbecue style on buns or over cornbread. The process shreds the meat which is not sliced or diced before cooking.

20	gallons water
¾	cup salt
½	cup black pepper
¼	cup sage
10	large red pepper pods
2	pork shoulders
1	beef brisket
1	large venison quarter or small goat
1	large possum (optional)
2	young groundhogs (optional)
2	yearling raccoons (optional)
12	large onions
6	chickens
4	rabbits
	Doves, quail and pheasants
20	ears corn, cut from cob, or 20 (16 ounce) cans whole kernel corn
1	gallon beer or 1 quart wine
20	tomatoes
20	potatoes, quartered
5	(16 ounce) cans lima beans
3	stalks celery, chopped
5	pounds yellow cornmeal

Kindle a good hardwood fire in a shallow pit in an open space, free of overhanging trees. Combine water and seasonings in large cast iron pot and bring to a full boil. Add pork, beef, venison, possum, ground-hog, raccoons and onions. Cook at a low boil for 2 to 3 hours. Add chicken, rabbits, game birds (whatever amount available) and corn. Allow fire to burn low enough to maintain a good simmer for 8 to 10 hours, stirring occasionally with a wooden ladle (a boat paddle works well). Avoid sticking; if ladle will stand upright in the mixture, add

Continued on next page

Kentucky Burgoo (continued)

water. Stir in liquor for flavor. The ingredients should cook to pieces with bones settling to the bottom during the last 6 hours of cooking time; clear pot often of bones and gristle. When 4 hours remain, add tomatoes, potatoes, beans and celery. Continue vigorous simmer, stirring until vegetables are thoroughly mixed. Check for consistency, adding water to thin or cooking down for thicker stew. Use cornmeal to prepare scalded cornbread.

Yield: 50 servings

Tom Pearce
Bowling Green, Kentucky

Broasted Swamp Rabbit

1   large swamp rabbit
     Salt and black pepper

Prepare a fire in a shallow hole, allowing coals to develop. Generously season rabbit with salt and pepper. Place on double thickness of aluminum foil and fold edges to form sealed packet. Remove coals from hole, place foil-enclosed rabbit in hole, cover with 1 inch dirt and replace coals over dirt layer. Cook for about 1½ hours, rekindling the fire if necessary to maintain sufficient heat. Remove rabbit.

If fresh corn is in season, shuck a couple ears, season with salt, pepper and butter, rewrap in green shucks and place in hole with rabbit to cook.

Yield: 2 servings

W. Horace Carter
Hawthorne, Florida

Cousin Ann's Brunswick Stew

2 or 3	squirrels
	Water
1	cup butter
1	(16 ounce) can cream style corn
1	(16 ounce) can lima beans
2	(16 ounce) cans sliced tomatoes
4	medium potatoes, peeled and cubed

Cook squirrel in stockpot with water to cover until meat separates from bones. Discard bones and return meat to cooking liquid which has been strained. Add vegetables and mix well. Bring to a boil over medium heat, then simmer for 2 to 3 hours. Add additional water if necessasry.

Yield: 6 servings

Ann Neely
Mayfield, Kentucky

Squirrel Bog

2	mature grey squirrels, cut up
2	quarts water
2	cups uncooked white rice
1	pound cured link sausage
	Salt and black pepper

Cook squirrel in water in stockpot until meat separates from bone. Discard bones and return meat to cooking liquid; add water if necessary to measure at least 4 cups. Add rice and sausage. Cook at a low boil for 30 minutes or until rice is tender and liquid is absorbed and evaporated. Season with salt and pepper.

Yield: 4 servings

W. Horace Carter
Hawthorne, Florida

Fricasseed Squirrel

4	squirrels, cut in serving-sized pieces
¾	teaspoon salt
	Black pepper
¼	cup all-purpose flour
4	slices bacon, cut in pieces
¼	cup sliced onion
½	cup chopped celery with leaves
2	teaspoons lemon juice
½	teaspoon thyme
1	beef-flavored bouillon cube
1	cup hot water

Rub squirrel pieces with salt and pepper; dredge in flour. In heavy skillet, fry squirrel with bacon until pieces are browned on all sides. Add onion, celery, lemon juice, thyme and bouillon which has been dissolved in hot water. Simmer, covered, for 1 hour. Check for tenderness.

Serve squirrel with hot regular or wild rice and broth.

Yield: 4 servings

Tim Tucker
Micanopy, Florida

Woodchuck in Slow-Cooker

1	medium-sized onion, thinly sliced
1 or 2	small woodchucks, cut in serving-sized pieces
1	(16 ounce) can tomatoes
1	(8 ounce) can tomato sauce
1	teaspoon salt
¼	teaspoon black pepper
1	teaspoon oregano
½	teaspoon basil
½	teaspoon celery seed
1	bay leaf
¼	cup dry red wine

Place onion in bottom of slow-cooker. Add meat, tomatoes, sauce, seasonings and wine. Cook, covered, on low setting for 8 to 10 hours. Remove bay leaf.

Serve woodchuck pieces with sauce over spaghetti.

Yield: 3 to 6 servings

Joan Cone
Williamsburg, Virginia

Harold's Wild Hog Loin

1	foot-long piece of inch-thick smoked sausage
1	foot-long piece of pork loin

Place sausage on a cookie sheet and freeze. With a long thin knife, push a hole all the way through the loin, lengthwise. Enlarge this hole with handle of wooden spoon. When the sausage is frozen hard, remove from the freezer and shove sausage into hole in the loin. Allow sausage to thaw before cooking. Grill loin, turning occasionally, over medium coals until well done—approximately one hour, but determine by testing meat, for heat varies with each cooker. Slice across loin.

Yield: serves 6

Harold Sanford
Bossier City, Louisiana

Mammy's Old Timey Possum

1   possum, cut in serving-sized pieces
       Salt
       Water
       All-purpose flour
       Black pepper
       Paprika
       Vegetable oil

Cook possum in lightly-salted water until tender. Remove from broth, reserving broth, and drain pieces. Dredge in flour seasoned with pepper and paprika. Fry in hot oil. Skim grease from broth and use to make gravy.

Serve possum and gravy with baked sweet potatoes.

Yield: 2 or 3 servings

Susan J. Sharpe
Hamlet, North Carolina

"If the sentimentalist were right, hunting would develop in men a cruelty of character. But I have found that it inculcates patience, demands discipline and iron nerve, and develops a serenity of spirit that makes for long life and long love of life. And it is my fixed conviction that if a parent can give his children a passionate and wholesome devotion to the outdoors, the fact that he cannot leave each of them a fortune does not really matter so much. They will always enjoy life in its nobler aspects without money and without price. They will worship the Creator in his mighty works. And because they know and love the natural world, they will always feel at home in the wide, sweet habitations of the Ancient Mother."

Archibald Rutledge

Fur and Feather Stew

3	squirrels or equivalent meat from any small game animal or upland bird
2	cups water plus moisture from thawing meat or 3½ to 4 cups water with fresh meat
3	medium carrots, diced
4	medium potatoes, diced
2	medium-sized onions, diced or whole
1	(2½ ounce) jar sliced mushrooms, drained
1	(8 ounce) can green beans, drained
1	(16 ounce) can whole kernel corn, drained
1	(8 ounce) can tomato sauce
1	cup ketchup
1	tablespoon sugar
2	teaspoons salt
1½	teaspoons black pepper
¼	teaspoon curry powder
2	bay leaves
2	teaspoons hot pepper sauce

Cook meat in water until it separates easily from bones. Remove from cooking liquid, bone and set meat aside. Simmer carrots and potatoes in broth for 15 to 20 minutes, then place vegetables and broth in slow-cooker. Add meat, remaining vegetables and seasonings. Cook on low setting for about 12 hours, stirring occasonally.

For quicker preparation, combine ingredients in large stockpot, instead of slow-cooker; cook for 1 to 1½ hours. Stew is especially good with hot cornbread.

Yield: 6 to 8 servings

Bob Kornegay
Blakely, Georgia

Sauteed Frog Legs

16	frog legs
	Dry white wine
1	bay leaf, crushed
	All-purpose flour
	Salt
	Black pepper
	Butter
½	cup sour cream
½	teaspoon dried onion flakes
2	tablespoons chopped parsley

Marinate frog legs overnight in wine with bay leaf. Drain and blot with paper towel. Dredge legs in flour seasoned with salt and pepper. Saute legs in butter in heavy skillet until golden brown; transfer to heated platter. Add sour cream, onion and parsley to skillet drippings. Mix well and bring to a near boil. Ladle over legs and serve hot.

Yield: 2 servings

Tim Tucker
Micanopy, Florida

"God created a great race of distinctive game birds and animals that are highly edible, and they are gifted peculiarly in wariness, craft, and speed. It appears to me reasonable to believe that, like so many other good gifts presented us by the Creator, He put game here to be hunted."

Archibald Rutledge

Wild Game Gumbo

This is a great way to clean out the freezer when a new hunting year begins with the traditional Plantation Dove Hunt. It takes all day and every pot in the house, but it's worth it!

2	quarts water
1	(2½ to 3 pound) chicken
1½	teaspoons salt
8	dove breasts
1	pound venison roast, cut into cubes
1	squirrel, quartered
1	rabbit, quartered
2	quail
1	small onion
1	stalk celery
1	bay leaf
1	tablespoon salt
¼	teaspoon red pepper
1½	pounds smoked link sausage, cut into ½-inch slices
¼	cup bacon drippings
½	cup all-purpose flour
1	cup chopped onion
1	cup chopped celery
2 - 3	teaspoons pepper
1	teaspoon hot sauce
½	teaspoon red pepper
1	teaspoon Worcestershire sauce
	Hot cooked rice

Combine 2 quarts water, chicken and 1½ teaspoons salt in a large Dutch oven and bring to a boil. Cover, reduce heat, and let simmer 1 hour or until tender. In another stockpot, place game, celery, onion, bay leaf, salt, and red pepper; cover with water and simmer until meat comes off bones. Remove meat from stock. Discard bones and strain broth. Set aside. Remove chicken from broth. Chill broth; skim fat from broth. Remove chicken from bones and chop meat into bite-size pieces. Set aside. Brown sausage in a large skillet over medium heat. Remove onto paper towels, leaving drippings in skillet. Add bacon drippings to skillet and heat over medium heat until hot. Add flour and cook, stirring constantly, until roux is the color of caramel (15 to

Continued on next page

Wild Game Gumbo (continued)

20 minutes). Add chopped onion, celery, and pepper; cook for 10 minutes. Combine roux and chicken broth in a large Dutch oven. Cover and simmer 30 minutes. Add game and chicken meat, sausage, hot sauce, red pepper, and Worcestershire sauce. Add reserved stock from game to make four quarts liquid. Simmer, uncovered, for 2 hours, stirring occasionally. Remove bay leaf. Serve gumbo over hot cooked rice.

Yield: 4½ quarts

Betsy Neill
Brownspur, Mississippi

"This privilege of hunting is about as fine a heritage as we have, and it needs to be passed on unsullied from father to son. There is still hope for the race when some members of it are not wholly dependent upon effete and urbane artificialities for their recreation....Hunting gives a man a sense of balance, a sanity, a comprehension of the true values of life that make vicious and crazily stimulated joy a repellent thing."

Archibald Rutledge

Red's Barbequed Raccoon

One of the most important steps in cooking a coon is in removing all the musk glands during skinning and cleaning. Be sure you have done so before starting this recipe, Red says.

1   raccoon, quartered
     Basil
     Oregano
     Tony Chachere's Cajun Seasoning (or suitable substitute)
     Worcestershire sauce
1   large onion
1   garlic clove
     Butter or margarine
     Barbeque sauce

Sprinkle meat heavily (or to taste) with basil, oregano, Cajun Seasoning, and Worcestershire sauce. Let sit for one hour. Cover coon pieces with water in large pot. Add onion and garlic, whole, to pot and bring to a boil. Turn heat down and let simmer for 3 hours, or until meat is tender. Remove while meat is still firmly attached to the bones. Water should still cover the meat. If necessary, add more water as it simmers. Let pot cool, uncovered, and then place in refrigerator overnight. Skim off fat and discard. Remove meat and pat dry. Place on grill over low heat and add hickory or pecan chips to the coals. Baste with butter and your favorite barbeque sauce. Cook slowly for about three hours, removing when meat begins to sag off the bones.

Yield: 1 large coon serves 2 couples

Red Reid Adams
Greenville, Mississippi

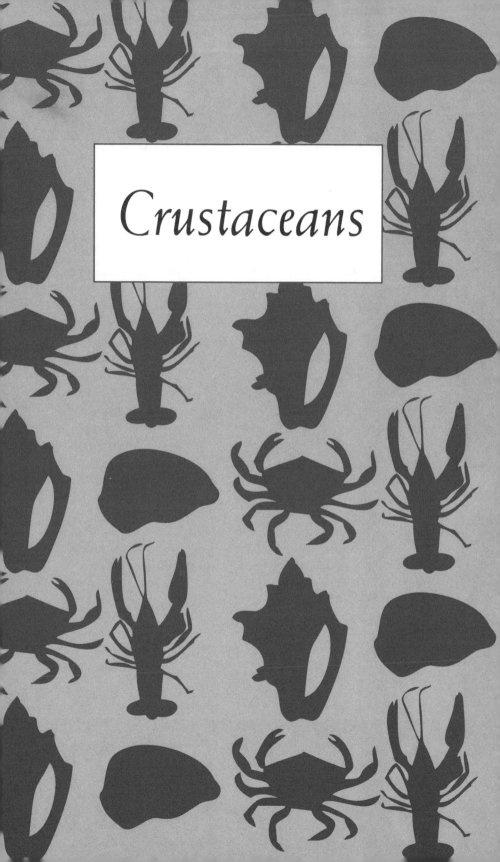

Crustaceans

Returnin' the Favor

Dad, you took me fishin' when I was just a freckle-faced boy;
Today those trips are treasured more than any remembered toy.
The swell times we spent together, no amount of gold could buy;
You were always so big an' strong—I was just a little guy
But you said we were "equal partners" right from the start;
I guess age doesn't matter much when measured from the heart.
Twenty-one years have passed since I grew up and left to stay....
Now, I've come to take you fishin', pay you back some small way.
I'll pick you up at sunrise, grinnin' in my fancy new rig....
Bass boats are mighty stylish now; we'll fool 'em with jig 'n pig.
Leave your readin' glasses home, I'll gladly tie all your baits;
My guidin' fees come cheap—you can easily afford the rates.
Dad, I only wish I'd come back sooner, my days are numbered too....
You were always my biggest hero, the best friend I ever knew.
Let's spend more time together, we don't even have to talk....
"Whoa!" This is where we start fishin', begin our silent stalk.
The first fish is yours, Dad, the second one too, if you like;
We'll catch us some big bass today, not bother with perch or pike.
But even if we go home fishless, it will all have been worthwhile.
Because I know you're happy, Dad; I saw it flashin' in your smile!
Next time I'll bring little Billy, it's time he learned a thing or two.
He's about the age I was when I first went out in a boat with you.
But, Dad, these moments are yours and mine to always share and
savor....
You took me fishin' as a boy—now I'm returnin' the favor.

Jim Martin

The Things That Grow Inside of Shells

According to the format of this collection of delightful delicacies, what follows is supposed to be a list of the most succulent ways to prepare the melange of somewhat hard-bodied creatures that inhabit the waters of Louisiana, gleaned from the refinement of generations of experience by the state's most touted cooks. In order to gain full appreciation of the development of these recipes, and realizing that present-day chefs can rapidly abandon the kitchen for a quick run to McDonald's if the outcome of the effort is not quite as expected, one must give full credit to those pioneers who couldn't and had to eat the end results—or go hungry. But the really amazing thing is how these forebears came to realize that these things were fit to eat in the first place.

Picture yourself, say, three hundred years ago, traipsing along an alligator trail in the Atchafalaya swamp with your trusty flintlock, hunting either supper, a hide for some new pajamas, or an Indian whose beads you could steal for the Saturday night buray game. Suddenly, you come across a 60-pound snapping turtle—big head, little feet, and M-60 tank-type armor. With a face like that, could you get hungry looking at it? Man, we think we're in a recession now…

Anyway, turtle soup and sauce piquant are presently staples and personally I can't get enough, mainly because I don't have to confront the critter on the half-shell—or cook it. Crabs are a different matter. I delight in catching, boiling, and eating these most tasty of salt-water crustaceans—that reflects how excessive exposure to the coastal sun adversely affects one's brain.

First of all, in catching a crab one exposes his fingers, toes, and other extremities to the beast's razor-sharp and vice-like pinchers—frequently. Secondly, if the cooking process is done with the crab still alive—as it should be, he does it all over again, in addition exposing his earlier wounds to hot, salty water. And finally he is left with something under three ounces of meat that takes something over an hour to decipher from gore and gills, dig out of a rock-hard skeleton, and consume. It's easy to understand why primal man ate the first—they'd eat anything. But it's beyond me why they ever ate the second, especially since they didn't have any crab boil back then.

Shrimp are an entirely different matter. Obviously, since the early settlers witnessed every wild creature from coons to sea gulls to speckled trout constantly feasting on them, they **had** to be good! It makes one wonder why so many different ways of cooking them have evolved over the centuries— like jambalaya, etouffe, bar-b-que, scampi (well, there **are** Cajun Italians!), and other exotic-sounding creations often followed by the innovator's name—that so efficiently mask the delicious delicacy of a shrimp. Maybe boiling them is the most recent discovery...

Conchs are another epicurean delight and a natural by-product of coastal oil fields, where they grow on platform pilings. Since our Acadian ancestors arrived long before the present-day plethora of conch-cultivators were constructed, it must be assumed that these creatures are a relatively new discovery. Whatever the case may be, a chef should be absolutely certain that he is boiling conch and not the hermit crabs that magically appear inside of the shell after the conch has died of natural causes. Surprises of that order are not good for the digestion.

But the most hard-bodied, ugliest, and tastiest of all—unless one happens to be a fanatical crawfish-connoisseur who suffers from the same brain ailment as a crab-lover—is the oyster. The man (or woman) who was brave enough to eat the first should be immortalized in the halls of momentous accomplishments—as should any present-day oyster-shucker who has accumulated less than two-dozen stitches from pocket-knife and screw-driver-induced gashes incurred while attempting to pry the stubborn things apart. Unfortunately, I do not qualify for this glorious honor, though I have determined that buying them by the gallon is cheaper than by the sack when you consider the associated medical bills.

Whatever, Louisiana has a lot of shelly creatures that are delicious almost any way that they are prepared. Thanks to the gastronomic fortitude of the pioneers, and the imaginations of generations of experimenters, the following are some of the best.

Pete Cooper, Jr.
Buras, Louisiana

Fried Softshell Crawfish

Fresh soft shelled crawfish
Eggs
Salt
Black pepper
Corn flour
Cornmeal
Cayenne pepper
Garlic powder
Allspice
Peanut oil

Clean fresh crawfish by removing top shell, eyes and calcium deposits above the eyes. Combine eggs, salt and pepper; pour over crawfish. Mix corn flour and cornmeal in 3:1 proportion; season with salt, cayenne pepper, garlic powder and allspice. Dip crawfish into corn flour mixture, place in hand-held strainer or colander and shake to remove excess flour, then place in peanut oil heated to 350 to 375 degrees; fry for about 3 minutes. Be careful to maintain oil heat between batches to avoid spattering or ignition.

Stephen Borne
Oak Alley Plantation, Louisiana

 "Fresh air and outdoor living do something to an angler's appetite; namely, bring out the glutton."

Charley Dickey

Softshell Crawfish Stir-Fry

1	clove garlic
¼	cup unsalted butter
16	softshell crawfish
1	medium-sized onion, chopped
1	medium-sized green bell pepper, chopped
12	small mushrooms, sliced
1	green onion, sliced
1	teaspoon seasoned salt
1	teaspoon Cajun seasoning
2	tablespoons white cooking wine

Clean crawfish by removing top shell, eyes and calcium deposits above the eyes; set aside. Saute garlic in butter in large skillet for 3 minutes. Remove garlic. Combine crawfish, vegetables, seasonings and wine in skillet. Saute for 3 minutes.

Serve crawfish over fettucine and garnish with parsley sprigs and lemon wedges.

Yield: 4 servings

Christy Sorenson
Livingston Parish, Louisiana

Stuffed Softshell Crawfish

24	fresh softshell crawfish
¼	cup butter
1	tablespoon all-purpose flour
½	cup minced onion
1	tablespoon minced garlic
½	cup chopped parsley
½	teaspoon salt
½	teaspoon black pepper
½	teaspoon red pepper
1	egg
4	cups white bread cubes or breadcrumbs
	Buttermilk
	All-purpose flour
	Vegetable oil

Clean crawfish by removing top shell, eyes and calcium deposits above the eyes. Reserving shells, remove meat, chop and set aside. Melt butter in skillet. Add flour and stir until lightly browned. Add onion and garlic; saute for a few minutes. Remove skillet from heat. Stir in parsley, seasonings, egg, bread and crawfish meat; mix well. Spoon about 2 tablespoons of mixture into crawfish shells. Dip shells into buttermilk, dredge in flour and fry in oil until golden brown.

Pour hollandaise sauce over shells before serving.

Yield: 5 or 6 servings

Colette Moreau Lottinger
Luling, Louisiana

Cohutta Mountain Crawdad Creole

Crawdad Creole should be attempted only with wild native crawdads, freshly taken from a tumbling mountain stream..and can be properly enjoyed only outdoors.

2 to 3	dozen (2 to 3 inch) North Georgia crawdads
1	cup canned mushrooms, undrained
1	medium-sized Vidalia onion, diced
½	cup margarine
½	cup all-purpose flour
1	cup water
¼	teaspoon thyme
1	bay leaf
	Dash cayenne pepper
	Salt and black pepper to taste
	Cooked rice

Cook crawdads in boiling water over campfire or campstove until bright red. Drain, cool to touch and shuck the meat from the tails. Drain mushrooms, reserving broth. Saute onion in margarine with mushrooms in saucepan for 3 minutes. Stir in flour and cook for 1 minute. Gradually add water and mushroom liquid, stirring con-stantly, and cook until thickened. Add seasonings and crawdad meat. Simmer for 5 minutes. Remove bay leaf and serve over rice.

Yield: 3 or 4 servings

Jimmy Jacobs
Mableton, Georgia

"Whether you are a fresh water Walton or plowing the depths for a long-billed mon-ster of the sea, you are seeking out the quiet aquatic spaces of the earth for a reason more compelling than to satisfy your stomach juices."

Charlie Elliott

Chicken with Clam Sauce

1 (2 pound) fryer chicken, cut in pieces
3 tablespoons olive or vegetable oil
   Salt
   Black pepper
1 (7½ ounce) can minced clams, undrained
1 (10¾ ounce) can cream of celery soup,
   undiluted

Saute chicken in oil until golden brown. Season with salt and pepper. Place chicken in 12x8x2-inch baking dish. Pour clams and soup over chicken. Bake, covered, at 325 degrees for about 1 hour or until chicken is tender.

If fresh clams are available, shuck them and grind flesh in meat grinder. Recipe requires about 1 cup of clams.

Yield: 4 servings

Paul Jennewein
Wrightsville Beach, North Carolina

White Clam Sauce for Pasta

¼ cup olive oil
½ cup butter or margarine
6 cloves garlic, minced
¼ cup minced parsley or flakes
1 tablespoon sweet basil
   Pinch of crushed red pepper
   Pinch of freshly ground black pepper
3 tablespoons grated Parmesan cheese
10 to 12 cherrystone clams, coarsely chopped, with juice
   or 2 (7½ ounce) cans chopped clams,
   undrained or 8 southern quahogs, ground with
   juice

Melt oil and butter together in saucepan. Add herbs and bring to a boil. Add clams and bring to a boil.

Serve clam sauce over spaghetti or noodles.

Yield: 3 or 4 servings

Paul Jennewein
Wrightsville Beach, North Carolina

Seafood Fettucine

1	pound medium shrimp, shelled and deveined
1	pound bay scallops, rinsed and blotted dry
½	pound fish fillet, skin and dark meat removed, and cut in bite-sized pieces
½	pound oysters (optional), rinsed and blotted dry
½	pound flaked fresh crabmeat
2	cups low-fat cottage cheese
½ to ¾	cup non-fat milk
2	cloves garlic (optional)
2	tablespoons all-purpose flour
½	teaspoon prepared mustard
1	tablespoon lemon juice
	Salt and freshly ground black pepper to taste
1 to 2	teaspoons parsley, basil, oregano or dill, or to taste
½	cup chopped onion (optional)
¼	large green bell pepper (optional), chopped
1	cup sliced or chopped fresh mushrooms
2	tablespoons butter or margarine, divided
¾	cup freshly grated Parmesan cheese (optional)
	White wine (optional)
1	(8 or 16 ounce) package fettucine
	Lemon slices or fresh herbs for garnish
1	tablespoon light olive oil
8 to 10	cherry tomatoes, cut in halves, or 1 tomato, seeded and chopped

After cleaning seafood, store each kind in separate covered container in refrigerator until sauce is prepared. Place cottage cheese, milk and garlic in blender container or food processor bowl; blend until smooth. Blend in flour. Add mustard, lemon juice, salt, pepper and herbs; blend well and set aside. Briefly saute onion, bell pepper and mushrooms in 1 tablespoon butter in skillet over medium heat. Add cheese mixture and cook until slightly thickened and flour is cooked; check for seasonings. Remove from heat and stir in Parmesan cheese and wine. Prepare fettucine according to package directions, cooked to al dente. Drain and place in serving dish; garnish with lemon slices or fresh herbs. Heat skillet or wok over medium heat, then add 1 tablespoon butter and olive oil. Saute shrimp for about 2

Continued on next page

Seafood Fettucine (continued)

minutes or until pink and no longer translucent; transfer to warm bowl. Saute scallops in skillet for 2 to 3 minutes or until no longer translucent. Transfer to bowl with shrimp, retaining scallop liquid in skillet. Reduce heat slightly and poach fish in stock. Transfer to bowl with other cooked seafood, retaining liquid in skillet. Cook to reduce liquid by about half, then cook oysters for 3 to 4 minutes or until sides curl; add with skillet liquid to other seafood. If omitting oysters, cook liquid to reduce liquid by about half, then pour over seafood. Combine crabmeat with cheese sauce and reheat. Add seafood and reheat quickly until steamy. Place in serving dish and garnish with tomatoes and lemon slices. Serve seafood and sauce over fettucine.

Good accompaniments include broccoli and a light lettuce salad with grapefruit and orange sections, avocado slices and a mayonnaise or blue cheese dressing.

Yield: 6 servings

Bea Baab
Augusta, Georgia

Squid Salad

5   pounds squid
    Water
3   stalks celery, chopped
    Dried black olives
¼   cup olive oil
    Juice of 1 lemon
    Salt and black pepper to taste
2   cloves garlic, chopped

In 5-quart saucepan, bring to a boil enough water to cover squid; add squid and cook just until squid turn white, about the amount of time until water comes to a second boil; do not overcook. Remove squid from water. Cut in ½-inch round slices. Combine squid, vegetables, oil, lemon juice, salt, pepper and garlic; toss to mix well. Chill for 2 to 3 hours.

Serve squid salad on lettuce leaf or as an appetizer.

Yield: 6 servings

Carmella Garitta
East Haven, Connecticut

Couscous Soup

1 ½	pounds farina
	Water
	Salt and black pepper
½	cup vegetable oil
1	clove garlic, minced
2	onions
5	pounds black fish
3	pounds clams
	Tomatoes, chopped
	Celery, chopped
	Carrots, diced

Place 2 handfuls farina on work surface and sprinkle with small amount of water. Work grain with fingers to separate and moisten evenly. Rake farina with 1 hand; with other hand, rub farina into small grains resembling lead shot. If mixture becomes too moist, add additional farina and begin again. Add farina and water until all grains are moistened; once or twice during process, place grains in a sieve and shake gently over a bowl. Spread farina still in sieve on table and let dry. Add salt, pepper, oil and garlic; mix and let dry. Devise a double broiler with a colander inset. Fill saucepan with water to about ¼ depth of pan. Insert colander and place 1 whole onion in colander, then add couscous. Steam, covered, for 2 to 3 hours. When onion is cooked, couscous is done. For soup, saute black fish and steam clams. Remove fish and clam meat and place juices and drippings in saucepan. Add water, vegetables, salt and pepper. Cook until vegetables are done. Add fish and clams; cook until tender. To serve, pour soup over couscous.

8 to 10 servings

Jennie Garitta
Lexington, North Carolina

Conch Seviche

2	pounds uncooked conch, cubed
2	cups lime juice
½	cup minced onion
¼	cup chopped green chilies
1	cup peeled, seeded and chopped tomatoes
2	teaspoons salt
	Few grains of cayenne pepper
⅛	teaspoon oregano

Combine all ingredients and place in baking dish. Chill, covered, for 3 to 4 hours with conch completely submerged in juice. Spoon into small scallop shells and serve with wooden picks.

Yield: 12 to 16 servings

Elise Vachon
Marietta, Georgia

Flagler Beach Coquina Soup

The best way to gather these little clams is to find several energetic youngsters who like to play in the sand and persuade them to dig up a bucket of the critters. If that fails, Jimmy Jacobs further suggests that tidal pools along the beach are sometimes a good source for the clams.

1	small bucket coquina clams
2	quarts water
½	cup margarine
1	(4 serving) packet instant mashed potatoes
	Salt and black pepper to taste

Combine coquina and water in saucepan; bring to a boil and continue to cook for about 10 minutes or until all shells are open. Drain and reserve broth; discard shells. Melt margarine in broth. Add potatoes and stir until dissolved. Season with salt and pepper.

Yield: 4 servings

Jimmy Jacobs
Mableton, Georgia

Crab Dip

When Sam Roberson was in Alaska, the waters abounded with plump, succulent Dungeness crab. "We could set a couple of crab pots and come up with a score or so of fat crab almost any time," he recalls. This dip was one way to use the crabmeat; the recipe also works with halibut cheeks, octopus, shrimp, crawfish or rattlesnake meat.

1   cup finely flaked crabmeat or 1 (6½ ounce) can crabmeat
2   tablespoons minced parsley
1   tablespoon minced onion
3   tablespoons mayonnaise
1   teaspoon lemon juice
¼   teaspoon curry powder
    Crackers

Combine crabmeat, parsley, onion, mayonnaise, lemon juice and curry powder; mix well. Chill before serving with crackers.

Yield: 6 servings

Sam H. Roberson
Lobelville, Tennessee

Crab Pate

1   (10½ ounce) can cream of mushroom soup, undiluted
1   envelope unflavored gelatin
3   tablespoons cold water
¾   cup mayonnaise (not salad dressing)
1   (8 ounce) package cream cheese, softened
½   pound fresh crabmeat
1   small onion, grated
½   cup chopped celery
    Parsley for garnish
    Crackers

Heat soup in saucepan over low heat; remove from heat. Dissolve gelatin in cold water in mixing bowl. Stir soup into gelatin. Add mayonnaise, cream cheese, crabmeat, onion and celery; mix well. Pour mixture into 4-cup mold. Chill until firm. Invert on serving plate and unmold. Garnish with parsley and serve with crackers.

Yield: 4 cups

James C. Wright, MD
Virginia Beach, Virginia

Mussels Steamed

36 fresh mussels
½ cup butter
1 clove garlic, crushed
1 teaspoon lemon juice
2 cups white wine

Using stiff bristle brush, scrub mud, sand and beard from mussels under cold running water; chill until ready to cook. Melt butter in small saucepan. Add garlic and lemon juice. Pour into small serving bowl for dipping. Pour wine into steamer and bring to a boil. Add mussels and steam until mussels open, usually ½ to 2 minutes. Discard mussels that do not open or smell right.

Serve mussels with French bread and white wine.

Yield: 2 entree or 12 appetizer servings

James C. Wright, MD
Virginia Beach, Virginia

"You are seeking many other things which add immeasurably more to your day than meat on the table. You're looking for sunshine on the water, the refrigerated glades, the bonds of fellowship between strong men."

Charlie Elliott

Oyster Stew

1   pint oysters with juice
1   quart milk, scalded
2   tablespoons butter or margarine
    Salt and black pepper to taste

Place oysters and juice in saucepan; heat until oyster edges curl. Add milk and simmer. Stir in butter and season with salt and pepper. Serve immediately.

Yield: 4 servings

Ginnie Jennewein
Wrightsville Beach, North Carolina

Oyster Stew for One

3⅓   tablespoons butter, divided
¼   teaspoon Worcestershire sauce
¼   teaspoon celery salt
6   large fresh oysters, juice reserved
1½   cups whipping cream (not half and half)
     Salt and black pepper to taste
     Oyster crackers

Place 3 tablespoons butter in microwave-safe bowl and cook on high setting until butter is melted and bubbling. Add Worcestershire sauce, celery salt and drained oysters; cook on high setting for 30 seconds. Stir in oyster juices and cream; cook on high setting for 30 to 40 seconds or until hot. Season with salt and pepper. Pour into serving bowl and float 1 teaspoon butter on soup. Serve with oyster crackers.

Yield: 1 serving

James C. Wright, MD
Virginia Beach, Virginia

Shrimp in the Shell

2 cups butter
2 cups vegetable oil
2 teaspoons fresh lemon juice
2 teaspoons minced garlic
1 teaspoon salt
2 teaspoons freshly ground black pepper
8 bay leaves, crushed
4 teaspoons rosemary
1 teaspoon basil
1 teaspoon oregano
1 teaspoon cayenne pepper
36 large shrimp
Hot pepper sauce
French bread

Melt butter in heavy ovenproof saucepan. Add oil and mix well. Stir in lemon juice, garlic and seasonings. Cook over medium heat, stirring frequently, until sauce begins to boil; reduce and simmer for 7 to 8 minutes, stirring frequently. Remove pan from heat and let stand, uncovered at room temperature, for at least 30 minutes. Add shrimp to sauce and mix well. Place pan over medium heat and cook shrimp for about 5 minutes or until they turn pink. Place pan of shrimp and sauce in oven and bake at 450 degrees for 10 minutes. To serve, pour about ½ cup sauce over individual servings of 6 shrimp. Offer hot pepper sauce and serve with warm French bread for dipping.

Yield: 6 servings

Colette Moreau Lottinger
Luling, Louisiana

Steamed Shrimp

¼ cup red wine vinegar
½ cup olive oil
4 green onions, chopped
1 large onion, chopped
½ stalk celery, chopped
2 lemons, cut in thick slices
Salt and black pepper to taste
Garlic powder to taste
4 pounds shrimp, heads removed but shells intact

Combine vinegar, oil, onion, celery, lemon and seasonings in large saucepot. Add shrimp and mix well. Simmer, covered, for about 45 minutes, stirring frequently.

Yield: 6 to 8 servings

Colette Moreau Lottinger
Luling, Louisiana

Hot Shrimp Dip

3 (8 ounce) packages cream cheese, softened
1 (12 ounce) carton small curd cottage cheese
2 (6½ ounce) cans shrimp, well drained and mashed
1 large tomato, diced
1 large onion, minced
1 (4 ounce) can green chilies, chopped and drained
3 pounds cooked shrimp, cut in chunks

Blend cream cheese and cottage cheese until smooth. Combine cheese, canned shrimp, vegetables and shrimp chunks in top of double boiler over gently boiling water. Heat thoroughly but do not cook as consistency will become too thin. Serve with chips or crackers.

Yield: 7 to 8 cups

Marjorie Walworth
Hephzibah, Georgia

Pickled Shrimp

½	cup chopped celery leaves
¼	cup whole mixed pickling spices
2	quarts boiling water
1 ½	pounds shrimp, shelled and cleaned
2	cups sliced onion
5	bay leaves
1 ½	cups vegetable oil
1 ½	cups white vinegar
¼	cup chopped pimiento
2	tablespoons capers in liquid
1 ½	teaspoons salt
1 ½	teaspoons celery seed
¼	teaspoon hot pepper sauce
	Salad greens

Enclose celery and pickling spice in cheesecloth bag, place in boiling water and simmer for 20 minutes. Add shrimp and simmer for 5 minutes. Drain. Arrange alternate layers of shrimp and onion in a bowl. Add bay leaves. Combine oil, vinegar, pimiento, capers, salt, celery seed and hot pepper sauce; mix well and pour over shrimp and onions. Chill, covered, for about 6 hours, stirring occasionally. Drain dressing and serve on salad greens.

Yield: 6 servings

Colette Moreau Lottinger
Luling, Louisiana

"The woods and streams hold many treasures. Some a man sees, some he feels, some are in his thoughts as he stands knee-deep in a pool, or relaxes by a nook that cradles the arm of his favorite lake."

Charlie Elliott

Junction's Stuffed Shrimp

1	large onion, minced
1	small green bell pepper, minced
2	stalks celery, minced
2	tablespoons prepared garlic
	Chopped parsley to taste
½	cup butter
2	pounds white crabmeat, flaked
2	cups seasoned breadcrumbs
2	pounds large shrimp, cleaned and butterflied
	Vegetable oil

Saute onion, pepper, celery, garlic and parsley in butter until vegetables are soft. Add crabmeat and simmer for 15 minutes. Stir in breadcrumbs and mix well. Spoon stuffing into shrimp. Fry shrimp in oil until golden brown.

Yield: 6 to 8 servings

Colette Moreau Lottinger
Luling, Louisiana

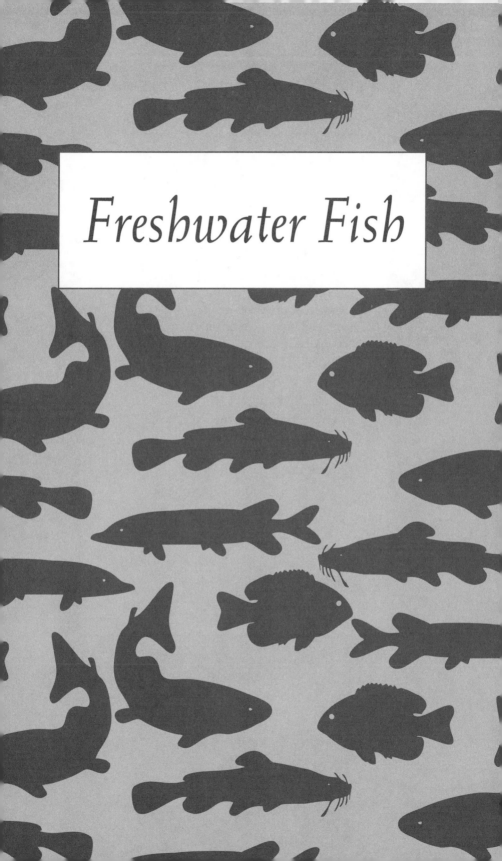

Freshwater Fish

Life's Like a River

Ever sat on the riverbank
    watching sticks float by?
It heals the soul, and calms the nerves;
    it does, but I don't know why.

Close your eyes and hear the river,
    it's all right to dream.
Cast your fears and worries out
    and float them down the stream.

Turtles sunning on a log,
    impervious to life.
They take things the easy way:
    no stress, no toil, no strife.

Learn a lesson from the river,
    with all its force and might.
It stays within its banks, you see,
    morning, noon and night.

Stay within your banks, my friend,
    and harbor no remorse.
God will give direction
    if you follow out His course.

Bob Anderson

Musings of an Angler

I cannot remember the first time I went fishing. Dad tells me that he took me to the lake behind the house. By his account, I caught crappie, or calico bass as we called them, until the minnows were all gone. And I didn't want to go home then.

Years later, having moved from Michigan to Virginia, it was my turn. My son Craig was just three years old. I had taken him fishing a few weeks earlier but it was a chilly spring day and he lost interest quickly, so we went home.

On a warmer day, we went fishing for bluegills. Or, as Dad observed, Craig fished while I baited hooks and took off the wiggling panfish that he caught, one after another.

Of course, not every trip has been so successful, at least as far as catching fish is concerned. In the fifty years that I have been a member of the fraternity of Izaak Walton, there doubtless have been as many trips when no fish were caught as when they were. As a means of providing food for the dinner table, angling as a sport is incredibly inefficient. Equipment, licenses, travel expenses and the host of miscellaneous costs far exceed the value of fish provided. That would be true even if catch and release had not become the practice.

Further, I frequently have been physically miserable when fishing. After I got a little older, I helped Dad gather bait in a white cedar swamp just south of town. The dirt was black and wet. Dad turned the earth and I grabbed the fat, blueish worms and popped them into a tin can. Mosquitoes also inhabited the swamp and I can recall how they stung my cheeks and hands. Bass fishing in the coastal Carolina streams or crossing the sand dunes on Pea Island to fish for tailor blues, the mosquitoes are every bit as plentiful and fierce as they were in that swamp.

I have been too hot, too cold, too wet while fishing. So has virtually every other angler.

Why, then, go fishing? It's hard to explain.

Fishing has provided a shared experience binding generations together. My dad taught me to fish. Then it was my turn to teach Craig, though now he is a young man and doing a good bit of teaching himself. Some of the best times fishing have been when the three of us went together. A dozen or so years ago, the three of us were after bass in Currituck Sound. Dad and I cast spinner baits over the milfoil while Craig sat in the corner of the boat indulging his newly discovered ability to read by devouring E.B. White's classic, *Charlotte's Web*. Though we were not keeping any of the bass, Craig always leapt up to net the fish. A fat two or three pounder latched onto my lure and Dad alerted Craig, "Get the net! Your dad's got a fish!" Craig didn't move. Again, "Craig, get the net! Hurry up!"

Craig stood up, still clutching his book. "I can't get the net now, Grandpa, I have to finish this paragraph!" We savor that exchange today.

In the summers, Craig and I often travel back to Michigan to fish for Northern Pike with Dad. We cram ourselves into his little aluminum boat and circle small lakes casting to weedbeds. When someone catches a fish, we yell and carry on like little kids. Actually, for a few moments, we are little kids. And each time we get together, we repeat the tales of earlier trips and share the expectations of the next one.

For me, fishing has also provided satisfaction in passing on skills and experiences to young folks besides Craig. Do you know how little is re-quired to become a hero to a youngster? And how profound the satisfaction?

Izaak Walton captured another of the spiritual values of fishing: "For Angling may be said to be so like the Mathematicks, that it can never be fully learnt; at least not so fully, but there will still be more new experiments left for the trial of other men that succeed us."

There is always a new trick to learn, some new observation to make. The key, as Sherlock Holmes once suggested to Dr. Watson, is to observe, not merely see. After all these years, I still have not got it all figured out. If I am lucky, I never will!

Walton, again, perhaps explained as well as anyone has in 300 years why fishing is so enjoyable: "In ancient times a debate has arisen, and it remains yet unresolved, whether the happiness of man in this world doth consist more in contemplation or action? ... Both these meet together, and do most properly belong to the most honest, ingenuous, quiet and harmless art of Angling."

Tim Mead
Charlotte, North Carolina

Beer Battered Bass

1½   pounds thin bass fillets
      Lemon juice
      All-purpose flour
      Salt and black pepper to taste
¼   cup vegetable oil
                    Batter
¾   cup all-purpose flour
¼   teaspoon salt
      Dash of black pepper
¾   cup beer

Cut fillets into 2-inch strips. Sprinkle with lemon juice and roll in flour seasoned with salt and pepper. Prepare batter by combining flour, salt and pepper, then gradually blend in beer, mixing thoroughly. Heat oil in heavy skillet. Dip fillets in batter and fry quickly in hot oil for about 2 minutes or until golden brown and fish flakes when probed with fork. Drain on paper towel to remove excess grease. Serve with tartar sauce.

Yield: 4 servings

Tim Tucker
Micanopy, Florida

Bass Eyes (or, Arkansas Lobster)

On a large bass, there is a good bite-sized chunk of meat right under each eye. Cut them out with a sharp knife and remove the skin. Salt heavily a potful of boiling water, and drop the pieces of bass (one may use cut-up fillets) into the boiling water. Cook until the fish is done, removing before the flesh becomes flaky. Five minutes is usually long enough, depending on the thickness of the pieces. Drain quickly on a paper towel and serve piping hot dipped in melted butter as hors d'oeuvres.

Gary Dye
El Dorado, Arkansas

Grilled Striper

1   whole striped bass, ½ to ¾ pound per serving
      Onion slices
      Green bell pepper slices
      Tomato slices
      Lemon slices
      Parsley sprigs
      Salt and black pepper to taste
      Butter

Prepare grill to produce very hot coals. Stuff fish with vegetable and lemon slices and parsley sprigs; season with salt and pepper. Pull edges together and secure with wooden picks. Place on well-buttered sheet of heavy-duty aluminum foil, fold to form a package and place on grill. Cover grill with grill lid or foil. Grill for 15 minutes, turn package and grill for additional 15 minutes. Check for doneness; fish at thickest point should flake when probed with fork.

Tim Tucker
Micanopy, Florida

Grilled Fish Picante

¾   cup low-calorie Italian dressing
2   cups picante sauce, hot or mild to taste,
        divided
2 to 3 pounds striper or hybrid fillets
½   cup sliced green onion
2   large tomatoes, diced
        Grated Parmesan cheese, to taste (optional)

Combine dressing and ¾ cup picante sauce; marinate fillets in mixture for 30 minutes. Prepare grill to produce hot coals or preheat broiler. Remove fillets from marinade. Grill over coals or broil on rack or foil-lined pan for 20 minutes per 1-inch thickness; do not turn very thin fillets. Serve topped with remaining picante sauce, onion, tomatoes and Parmesan cheese.

Yield: 6 to 8 servings

Howard P. Lindsey
Bowling Green, Kentucky

Baked Fish with Dressing

2	pounds spottail bass, hybrid or striper fillets, skin removed
2	cups stale home-style bread cubes or pieces
½	cup chopped onion
½	cup chopped celery
1	egg
½	cup milk
1	teaspoon poultry seasoning
	Salt to taste
	Freshly ground black pepper
½	cup melted butter
1 to 2	tablespoons lemon juice

Rinse fillets in cold water, blot with paper towels and place in single, flat layer in greased baking pan or dish; pan may be prepared with non-stick vegetable spray. Combine bread, onion, celery and egg. Add just enough milk to thoroughly moisten the bread. Sprinkle with seasonings and mix well. Spoon dressing evenly over fillets. Combine butter and lemon juice; pour over dressing. Bake at 350 degrees for 20 minutes or until dressing is lightly toasted and fish flakes when probed with fork.

Crabmeat may be added to the dressing and used on fillets or to stuff shrimp; stuffed shrimp will require shorter baking time.

Yield: 4 servings

Bea Baab
Augusta, Georgia

"To catch a fish may be the impulse that brought him to the witchery of waters, from which he gleans a harvest of moments not in any way connected with a fish."

Charlie Elliott

Largemouth Bass Hoka

One night while they lived in Oxford, Mississippi, Jim and Malinda McCafferty were watching a movie in the Hoka, an old cotton gin warehouse turned art theatre, one of that little city's more famous landmarks, along with William Faulkner's home. In the middle of the movie, the aroma of barbecued shrimp drifted through from the Moonlight Cafe, an eatery run on the Hoka's premises by its proprietor, Ron Shapiro. McCafferty began wondering how largemouth bass would taste if done up in the style of barbecued shrimp. Borrowing from a number of shrimp recipes, the couple came up with a marinade they thought would do justice to the bass and similar fish. The creation was a success and they named it in honor of the Hoka which, in addition to being the name of the theatre cafe, was the name of the Chickasaw Indian lady who had held title to much of the land upon which Oxford lies.

¼	cup plus 1 tablespoon lemon juice
¼	cup plus 1 tablespoon olive oil
2	tablespoons melted butter
2	tablespoons Worcestershire sauce
2	teaspoons hot pepper sauce
2	teaspoons garlic powder
½	teaspoon salt
2½	pounds bass or other fish fillets

Combine lemon juice, oil, butter, sauces and seasonings. Marinate fillets overnight. Place in baking dish in single layer. Bake at 350 degrees for 30 to 40 minutes or until fish is white and flakes easily when probed with fork.

Yield: 4 servings

Jim McCafferty
Ridgeland, Mississippi

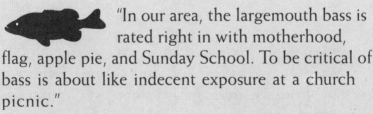

"In our area, the largemouth bass is rated right in with motherhood, flag, apple pie, and Sunday School. To be critical of bass is about like indecent exposure at a church picnic."

Charley Dickey

Oven Broiled Bass

8	slices bacon
1	medium-sized onion, chopped
1½	cups diced apple
2	lemons, thinly sliced
1	green bell pepper, chopped
1	4 to 5 pound bass, cleaned but skin intact
1	tablespoon salt
1	teaspoon pepper
¼	cup butter
¾	cup Worcestershire sauce
1	teaspoon garlic powder
1	teaspoon celery salt

Place 4 bacon slices in bottom of shallow baking pan. Combine onion, apple, lemon slices and green pepper; layer one-third of mixture on bacon slices. Sprinkle both sides of fish with salt and pepper; place on vegetable mixture. Spoon one-third of mixture into fish cavity and remaining one-third on top of fish. Melt butter in small saucepan, stir in Worcestershire sauce, garlic powder and celery salt, and bring to a boil; remove from heat. Use butter mixture to baste fish while baking. Bake at 375 degrees for about 1 hour or until fish separates from bones; do not turn fish. Serve hot.

Dish may be assembled in advance and refrigerated until time to bake.

Yield: 4 to 5 servings

Pam Strickland
Natchez, Mississippi

Charcoal-Broiled Bass

Removing the skin from a bass will improve the flavor of the meat immeasurably. Don't try this recipe without doing so.

1	large bass (3 to 6 pounds)
¼	pound butter or margarine
⅔	cup Worcestershire sauce
¼	cup lemon juice concentrate
¼	teaspoon Tabasco Sauce

Remove head and fins from cleaned bass, and skin the fish. Melt butter or margarine over low heat, stirring in lemon juice and Worcestershire sauce. Add Tabasco and simmer for five minutes. Use this as a baste sauce. As coals begin to turn gray, place bass on grill to cook, turning frequently with a large spatula and basting even more frequently. Add a few more pieces of charcoal to the fire if needed. If the fire is too hot, the meat will stick to the grill. Cook until the meat begins to flake. When you think the flesh is fixing to fall through the grill, it is done. A 5 pound bass takes about 45 minutes to cook. Reheat baste sauce, and pour over the bass on the serving platter.

Robert Hitt Neill
Brownspur, Mississippi

Rock Fish Nuggets

4	striped bass fillets
1	egg
¼	cup milk
	Packaged seafood mix
2	cups vegetable oil

Remove any red meat from fillets; cut fillets in 2-inch squares. Beat egg and milk together. Dip fillet pieces into egg liquid, place in bag containing seafood mix and shake well. Fry fish in oil heated to 350 degrees; squares will float to surface when cooked. Serve with hushpuppies and slaw.

Yield: 4 servings

Glenn Kimbrell
Burlington, North Carolina

Scales Down Smoked Fish

4	bass, redfish, striped bass or hybrid bass fillets, scales and skin intact
1½	cups dry white wine
5½	teaspoons crushed tarragon, divided
1	tablespoon Worcestershire sauce
	Cracked black pepper to taste
	Salt to taste
	Cayenne pepper (optional)
	Drawn butter
	Fresh lemon juice

When preparing fillets, remove rib cages but leave scales and skin attached. Combine white wine, 4½ teaspoons tarragon, Worcestershire sauce and cracked black pepper in baking pan or dish large enough to contain fillets in single layer. Place fillets, meat side down, on seasonings. Chill for 2 to 5 hours. Remove fillets from refrigerator 30 minutes before cooking; remove from pan to bring them to room temperature. Prepare grill, suitable for smoking, to provide hot coals. Season fillets with salt, additional black pepper, 1 teaspoon tarragon and cayenne pepper. Place, scale side down, on grill and cook for 4 minutes. Add hickory chips, mesquite chips or grapevine to coals, close grill for smoking and cook for 10 minutes; do not overcook. The scales and skill form a seal to hold the fillets intact and prevent sticking/drying; do not turn. Remove fillets from grill. Use fillet knife, starting at tail end and sliding blade forward to remove scales and skill. Serve with basting sauce of drawn butter and lemon juice.

Yield: 4 servings

Robert H. Cleveland Jr.
Brandon, Mississippi

"When you meet a buddy just back from a week's fishing trip, and he starts by talking about the beautiful scenery, you know he didn't catch any fish."

Charley Dickey

Mock Lobster Casserole

2	pounds bass fillets
1	lemon
	Salt to taste
1	(10¾ ounce) can cream of shrimp soup, undiluted
¼	cup chopped onion
2	cloves garlic, sliced
¼	cup margarine
2	teaspoons Worcestershire sauce
1	cup bread cubes or ¾ cup crushed crackers
	Cheddar cheese, thinly sliced

Place fillets in well-buttered 2-quart casserole or baking dish. Squeeze lemon over fillets, removing any seeds. Season with salt. Spread soup over fillets. Bake, uncovered, at 375 degrees for 30 minutes. During baking time, saute onion and garlic in margarine. Remove from heat and stir in Worcestershire sauce and bread cubes or cracker crumbs. Removed baked fillets from oven and stir until fish is flaked and evenly blended with soup. Sprinkle bread mixture over soup and fish. Bake, uncovered, for an additional 10 minutes. Top with cheese slices and broil until cheese is melted.

Yield: 6 servings

Jim McCafferty
Ridgeland, Mississippi

"Suddenly — the music came! The whipping crescendo was like a million violins in some mighty orchestra. It faded and came again, with its boom of thunderous drums in the background. From the tinkle of the little rivulet where I sat, to the harmonious fury of the opaque world outside, I had found the music of the elements!" (When caught in a storm while trout fishing.)

Charlie Elliott

Lobster Facade

Looks and tastes like lobster—excellent as an appetizer.

Striped Bass (Rock Fish)
1 ½ quarts water
1 teaspoon salt
1 ounce liquid seafood seasoning or ½ cup
   regular seafood seasoning

Filet fresh bass, remove rib cage and skin and make sure fish is completely deboned. Place filets on cutting board with outside in up position exposing lateral line and dark tissue. Remove dark meat with sharp filet or electric knife by making a thin slice, about ¹⁄₁₆-inch deep, the length of the filet. Make sure all dark flesh area is removed and cut filets into bite-size squares. Fill a two-quart saucepan with 1½ quarts water, add salt and seafood seasoning. Heat water until small bubbles appear. Do not bring to a full boil. Add diced filets and boil slowly for two to three minutes, being careful not to overcook or allow fish to crumble. Serve warm with garlic-seasoned drawn butter or chill and serve with seafood cocktail sauce.

Carle Dunn
Zwolle, Louisiana

Bluegill with Mustard

4 bluegill fillets
   Prepared mustard
   Salt and black pepper to taste
1 tablespoon olive oil
1 tablespoon butter

Lightly spread each fillet with mustard; season with salt and pepper. Saute in oil and butter over medium heat, cooking each side for a few minutes, depending on fillet thickness. Fish should flake when probed with fork; do not overcook.

Yield: 4 servings

Joann and William F. Black
Greensboro, North Carolina

South Edisto River White Catfish Stew

5	pounds catfish, dressed weight
½	pound bacon, diced
3	pounds Irish potatoes, diced
2	pounds onions, diced
4 to 5	cups water
6	hard-cooked eggs, diced
1	(4 ounce) can pimiento, drained and diced
1	(6 ounce) can evaporated milk
	Salt and black pepper to taste

Fry fish, using own preferred method, until fish flakes when probed with fork; remove bones. Fry bacon until crisp; remove from skillet and set aside. Fry potatoes and onion in bacon drippings until tender. Place fish in 4 cups water in soup pot; bring to a boil. Add bacon, potatoes, onion, eggs and pimiento. Simmer for 1 to 1½ hours, adding water if necessary but stew should be thick. Just before serving, stir in milk and season with salt and pepper. Unlike a tomato-based fish stew, white stew is not usually served over rice. Stew may be frozen and reheated.

Yield: 7 to 8 servings

Pat Williams
Santee, South Carolina

Broiled Sac-a-Lait

Sac-a-Lait is the Cajun term for crappie, taken from the French for "bag of milk." Other aliases include white perch, papermouth, bachelor perch, strawberry bass, speckled perch and in South Florida, specks.

Sac-a-lait fillets
Melted butter
Lemon juice
Salt and black pepper to taste
Tarragon to taste

Arrange fillets on broiler pan. Baste with butter and lemon juice and season with salt, pepper and tarragon. Broil or bake until tender; do not turn. Moisture rising on top of the fillets indicate it is being overcooked.

Jerald Horst
Louisiana Cooperative Extension Service

Fort Motte Red Catfish Stew

5	pounds catfish (fillets preferred), dressed weight
2	pounds butts meat, diced
2	pounds onions, diced
	Salt and black pepper to taste
1	tablespoon sugar
5	(10¾ ounce) cans tomato soup, undiluted
2	medium potatoes, diced

Place fillets in soup pot with water to cover; bring to a boil. Fry butts meat thoroughly, remove from cooking grease and add to soup pot. Cook onions in butts meat grease until brown, remove and add to soup pot. Stir in salt, pepper, sugar and canned soup. Simmer for 15 to 20 minutes. Separately cook potatoes in water to cover until tender; drain and add to soup pot a few minutes before stew is done.

Yield: 7 to 8 servings

Pat Williams
Santee, South Carolina

Sac-a-Lait (Microwave)

Sac-a-Lait fillets
Thinly sliced onion
Lemon juice
Butter (optional)
Fish seasoning

Place fillets in microwave-proof casserole or baking dish. Arrange onion slices on fillets. Drizzle lemon juice and butter over onion and sprinkle with seasoning. Cover with plastic wrap. Cook on High for a few minutes; let stand, covered, until fluffy. Onions will be firm and crunchy; precook them if soft texture is preferred. Sac-a-lait are tender and should not be used in a courtbouillon.

Colette Moreau Lottinger
Luling, Louisiana

Deep Fried Sac-a-Lait

Sac-a-lait fillets
1   egg
½   cup milk
1   teaspoon crab boil
Fish fry mix or seasoned cornmeal
Vegetable oil

Place fillets in casserole or baking dish. Blend egg, milk and crab boil; pour over fillets. Marinate, covered, overnight in refrigerator. Remove from marinade, dip in fish fry or cornmeal mix and fry in hot oil.

Mike Roy
St. Charles Parish, Louisiana

Jules' Fried Fish

Fish fillets or well scaled and cleaned small fish
Fish fry mix or seasoned cornmeal
Vegetable oil

Dredge fillets or fish in fish fry or cornmeal mixture. Fry in very hot oil for crispness; fish should flake when probed with fork. Drain on brown paper bags.

Jules Moreau
Marksville, Louisiana

Colette's Pan Fried Fish and Salsa

	Large sac-a-lait fillets
	All-purpose flour
	Salt and black pepper to taste
	Olive oil
	Butter
	Lemon slices
	Parsley sprigs
1	ripe tomato, grated
½	jalapeno pepper, grated

Sprinkle fillets with flour, salt and pepper. Fry in small amount of blended oil and butter in non-stick skillet; quickly brown one side, turn and brown the other side until fish flakes when probed with fork. Serve with lemon slice and parsley sprig or with spoonful of salsa, made by mixing tomato and jalapeno pepper.

Colette Moreau Lottinger
Luling, Louisiana

"Fish taken out of the water and fried on the riverbank are many times more delicious than those bought at the supermarket. An oak fire, the smell of pine woods, the soft breeze — all seem to add flavor that cannot be obtained under a roof."

Charlie Elliott

Baked Crappie with Red Rice

2	cups regular white rice
8	slices bacon
1	large onion, chopped
1	green bell pepper, chopped
1	(15 ounce) can tomato sauce
3 to 4	pounds speckled perch (crappie) fillets
	Lemon juice

Prepare rice according to package directions. Fry 4 slices bacon until crisp; remove from pan, break into small pieces and set aside. Saute onion and pepper in bacon drippings until tender. Combine vegetables, rice, bacon pieces and tomato sauce; spread mixture in shallow baking dish. Arrange fillets on rice, sprinkle with lemon juice and place remaining bacon slices over fillets. Bake at 350 degrees for 1 hour or until fish flakes when probed with fork.

Yield: 4 to 6 servings

Tim Tucker
Micanopy, Florida

"The white moon hung like a stage light, casting its brilliance on the falls. I jumped a rivulet to an enormous boulder...and gazed upward to a hundred foot veil of water that floated sheer into a deep blue pool. I forgot the fish, and even about putting my rod together."

Charlie Elliott

Crappie with Wild Rice Stuffing

6	crappie, filleted
1	teaspoon salt
1 ¼	teaspoons black pepper, divided
1	(6 ounce) package long grain and wild rice mixture with seasoning
½	cup chopped onion
½	cup chopped celery
1	(2 ½ ounce) can mushrooms, drained
¼	cup butter or margarine
¼	cup chopped parsley
	Vegetable oil

Blot fillets to remove moisture; season all sides with salt and 1 teaspoon pepper. Prepare long grain and wild rice mixture according to package directions, cooking onion, celery and mushrooms in butter until tender. Stir in parsley and ¼ teaspoon black pepper and mix thoroughly. Spoon stuffing loosely into each fillet, place in well-greased baking pan and brush with oil. Bake, basting occasionally with oil, at 350 degrees for 25 minutes or until fish flakes easily when probed with fork.

Yield: 6 servings

Tim Tucker
Micanopy, Florida

Crappie Chowder

3 or 4	crappie, skin removed and boned
1	onion, diced
1	green bell pepper, diced
¼	pound bacon, diced
1	(10¾ ounce) can cream of potato soup, undiluted
1	(16 ounce) can corn
1	(16 ounce) can diced carrots
3	small potatoes, diced
	Salt and black pepper to taste
1	soup can milk

Cut crappie into small pieces; chill until ready to use. Saute onion and green pepper with bacon until bacon is crisp. Combine bacon and vegetable mixture, potato soup, corn, carrots, potatoes and fish pieces in large saucepan; season with salt and pepper. Simmer for 30 minutes or until fish flakes when probed with fork. Stir in milk just before serving.

Yield: 4 or 5 servings

Tim Tucker
Micanopy, Florida

"A true sportsman is one who can catch a large fish, release it, and never tell anyone."

Charley Dickey

Creamy Crappie Dip

2 pounds crappie, dressed weight
3 cups boiling water
1 tablespoon salt
1 cup small curd cottage cheese
1 (8 ounce) carton sour cream or yogurt
½ cup shredded carrot
¼ cup chopped sweet pickle, drained
1 tablespoon chopped pimiento
1 tablespoon horseradish
2 teaspoons salt
   Chopped parsley

Place fish in boiling water seasoned with 1 tablespoon salt; reduce heat and simmer, covered, for 8 to 10 minutes or until fish flakes easily when probed with fork. Drain and let stand to cool. Remove skin and bones; flake and chill until ready to use. Combine cottage cheese, sour cream, carrot, pickle, pimiento, horseradish and 2 teaspoons salt; mix well. Stir in flaked fish. Chill for several hours. Sprinkle with parsley. Serve with chips, crackers or raw vegetables.

Yield: 4 cups

Tim Tucker
Micanopy, Florida

Garfish Delight

    1   garfish (30 inches or longer)
         Salt and black pepper to taste
         Boiling water
    ½   cup butter or margarine, melted

Cut garfish open from gills to tail and break back the rib cage, exposing the backbone. Using a sharp knife, remove the strip of boneless white tenderloin on each side of the backbone. A 30-inch garfish will produce a piece about ¾ inch in diameter and 20 inches long. Wash meat and cut in 1-inch pieces. Season with salt and pepper. Cook in boiling water for about 5 minutes or until tender.

Dip fish chunks in melted butter to eat.

Glenn Lau of Ocala, Florida, uses an ice cream scoop to remove the tenderloin instead of peeling it out in strips. He refers to the delicacy as "gar balls."

Yield: 3 or 4 servings

W. Horace Carter
Hawthorne, Florida

Chain Pickerel Steaks

    2   (2 pound or larger) chain pickerel or jackfish
    1   cup white cornmeal
    ½   cup self-rising flour
         Salt and black pepper to taste
         Corn or peanut oil

Scale and clean the pickerel, removing the head and tail and washing thoroughly. Using heavy, sharp knife, cut through backbone, slicing to produce thin steaks about¼-inch thick (no thicker than 3/8 inch). Mix cornmeal with flour in plastic bag or paper sack. Season the fish slices with salt and pepper or add seasonings to cornmeal mixture. Drop slices into bag and shake until well coated. Fry in hot oil in skillet deep enough to float the fish slices; remove when browned and serve immediately. The y-bones will be crisp enough to eat; remove the easy to find backbone.

Yield: 3 or 4 servings

W. Horace Carter
Hawthorne, Florida

Minnows on the Rocks

Not recommended for gourmets or those with sensitive stomachs, dried minnows can be palatable and sometimes even mean the difference between death and survival. The story and instructions from Dr. John N. Hamlet, a naturalist from Rapid City, South Dakota (deceased in Mayport, Florida, in 1981) recall a youthful experience. While living with the Sioux Indians in South Dakota, he and a 14-year-old Indian companion were tested by tribal leaders. They were sent into the desolate Black Hills for 10 days and challenged to live off the land with only the meager tools of a pen knife and a 1-yard piece of string. If they lost weight during the test, they were to be severely punished. Minnows were plentiful in the shallow, clear mountain streams. Hamlet and his friend flailed the water with sticks until the stunned minnows floated to the surface. They scooped the small fish up in their hands, spread them in the bright sunshine and let them dry. Dr. Hamlet said they were reasonably tasty but more importantly, nutritious and much more so than the jackrabbits they'd snared with their string. And the boys kept their health and weight throughout the 10-day test.

W. Horace Carter
Hawthorne, Florida

Roasted Minnows

Stone-toters and other small fish that are plentiful in the creeks and branches of the South can be appetizing and nutritious although it does take patience to dress and prepare them. Sprinkled with salt and pepper, their flavor can match that of mountain-stream trout.

12   minnows
Salt and black pepper to taste

Scale, clean, remove heads and wash the minnows well. Season with salt and pepper. Spread on a screen above a hardwood fire. Cook for 5 to 10 minutes or until done.

Yield: 1 serving

W. Horace Carter
Hawthorne, Florida

Court Trout

A European dish that transforms boiled fish into an entree fit for any royal house, this method is credited to Mrs. C.P. Jennewein, a native of Rome, Italy. In addition to gray and speckled trout, the process may be used on croakers, sheepsheads, drum and whiting.

1½	gallons water
1	cup wine vinegar
1	stalk celery
½	carrot
¼	medium-sized onion
½	cup salt
2	bay leaves
4 or 5	peppercorns
1	(3 pound) speckled trout, cleaned and scaled but head intact

Combine water, vinegar, vegetables and seasonings in large pot. Bring to a boil and cook for 30 minutes. Reduce heat and add whole fish. Cover tightly. Cook for 10 minutes, turn heat off, and let stand for 10 additional minutes or until fish eyes are opaque. Serve hot. To serve cold, store on a platter with ½-inch broth (which will form gelatin) in the refrigerator.

Yield: 3 or 4 servings

Paul Jennewein
Wrightsville Beach, North Carolina

"One reason for using a professional guide is that when you don't catch any fish, the guide can tell you a lot of good stories, especially about the monsters his previous customers caught."

Charley Dickey

Baked Trout in Foil

3 or 4	(¾ to 1 pound) trout or catfish, dressed weight
1	clove garlic, crushed
¼	cup margarine, softened
1	teaspoon salt
⅛	teaspoon black pepper
½	teaspoon dried thyme
1	teaspoon all-purpose flour
½	pound shelled, deveined large shrimp
½	pound mushrooms, sliced
3	tablespoons lemon juice
½	cup cooking wine
¼	cup chopped parsley
1	teaspoon grated lemon peel

Wash whole fish, inside and out, under cold running water. Blot with paper towels to dry well. Combine garlic, margarine, seasonings and flour. Place fish on double thickness of heavy duty aluminum foil. In cavity of each, place ½ teaspoon of garlic mixture, 2 shrimp and ¼ cup mushrooms. Sprinkle with ½ teaspoon lemon juice and 1 teaspoon wine. Use remaining garlic mixture to dot top of each fish and arrange remaining shrimp and mushrooms on fish. Sprinkle with remaining lemon juice, wine, parsley and lemon peel. Bring long sides of foil sheet together over fish and secure with double fold; fold foil ends upward several times and place on baking sheet. Bake at 375 degrees for 45 minutes, allowing 10 to 12 minutes per pound, or until fish flakes easily when probed with fork. Serve on heated platter with juices spooned over fish.

To prepare on a grill over an open fire, grill foil-wrapped fish for 15 minutes, turn, grill another 15 minutes, and check for doneness; grill for additional 15 minutes per side if necessary.

Yield: 4 servings

John and Denise Phillips
Fairfield, Alabama

Dishwasher Salmon

Restaurants in Soldotna on the Kearni River in Alaska use this cooking method. Salmon is especially delicious.

> Salmon, small trout, bass, catfish or other fish
> fillets
> Sweet and sour dressing
> Juice of 1 lemon
> Mayonnaise
> Salt and black pepper to taste
> 1 (10½ ounce) can shrimp soup

Lightly brush fresh fillets with dressing and lemon juice. Let stand at room temperature for 2 to 3 hours. Fold aluminum foil into 2 boat shapes for each fillet. Place each fillet in a boat, brush lightly with mayonnaise and season with salt. Crimp edges to prevent leakage from top and sides and place second boat over fish, crimping and folding edges. Place boats in dishwasher. Set at highest temperature (up to 180 degrees) and run for one cycle, up to 20 minutes. Leave in dishwasher until ready to serve. Season with pepper or Cajun or other seasonings. Heat shrimp soup, seasoned with black pepper, and serve as sauce with fillets.

Fish with especially soft flesh is cooked with skin intact, then filleted after cooking. Other salad dressings may be used.

J. Ray Chapman
North Charleston, South Carolina

Baked Fish with Basil

6	white flesh fish fillets
	Salt and black pepper to taste
1	tablespoon basil
2	tomatoes, diced
2	green bell peppers, diced
1	large onion, diced
½	cup melted butter or margarine

Arrange fillets in single layer in baking dish. Season with salt, pepper and basil. Arrange tomatoes, peppers and onions over fillets. Pour butter over fillets and vegetables. Bake at 325 degrees for 30 minutes or until fish flakes easily when probed with fork.

Good accompaniments include a broccoli-cauliflower salad, rice pilaf, crusty French bread and a white zinfandel wine.

Yield: 3 or 4 servings

Tony Mullis
Denton, North Carolina

Foil Fish

1	serving halibut, catfish, flounder, trout or bass
2 to 3	teaspoons lemon juice
2 to 3	tablespoons butter
	Salt and black pepper to taste
	Parsley, basil or dill sprigs

Preheat oven to 350 degrees or prepare outdoor grill to produce hot coals. Place fish in center of 12-inch aluminum foil square. Drizzle lemon juice and butter over fish and add seasonings. Fold edges of foil to form tightly sealed packet. Grill or bake for 15 minutes.

Fresh vegetables may be enclosed with fish in packet.

Yield: 1 serving

Elise Vachon
Marietta, Georgia

Baked Fish

Buck Paysour, author of Tar Heel Angler, Bass Fishing in North Carolina and Bass Fishing in North Carolina (revised), gives credit for this recipe to fishing buddy Bob Harned "who apparently got it from somebody else."

      ½   cup sliced onion
      ¼   cup butter or margarine
      ¾   teaspoon salt
             Black pepper to taste
      1 ½   cups soft breadcrumbs
             White perch, yellow perch, largemouth bass,
             striped bass, flounder or other fish fillets
             Grated Parmesan cheese
      ¾   cup milk

Saute onions in butter until lightly browned. Season with salt and pepper; add breadcrumbs. Arrange fillets in baking dish. Spoon crumb mixture on top of fillets. Sprinkle generously with cheese. Pour milk around fillets. Bake at 350 degrees for 45 minutes.

Bottom of baking dish can be lined with soft bread slices. Breadcrumb mixture can also include ½ cup grated Cheddar cheese. Strong flavored fish should be marinated overnight in wine or lemon juice.

Buck Paysour
Greensboro, North Carolina

Baked Fish Parmesan

Sam Roberson claims that "this is the best way I know to fix fish if you can't fry it...it works for most any fish I've ever caught."

             Fish fillets
      2   (8 ounce) cans tomato sauce
             Grated Parmesan cheese

Arrange fillets in single layer in baking dish. Pour tomato sauce over fillets to cover. Sprinkle generously with cheese, then sprinkle again. Bake at 350 degrees for about 20 minutes per inch thickness of fillets.

Sam Roberson
Lobelville, Tennessee

Fish in Foil

2	cups sliced mushrooms
¼	cup butter, divided
1	(8 ounce) carton sour cream
½	cup mayonnaise
	Salt and black pepper to taste
2	pounds crappie, walleye, bream, bass or catfish fillets
½	lemon
	Paprika

Saute mushrooms in 2 tablespoons butter until soft. Drain, then combine with sour cream, mayonnaise, 2 tablespoons melted butter, salt and pepper. Place each fillet in center of aluminum foil square. Squeeze lemon over fillets and top with spoon of sour cream mixture. Fold edges of foil to form tighly sealed packet. Bake at 350 degrees for 20 minutes, unwrap and broil for 1 minute. Sprinkle with paprika.

To prepare on outdoor grill, place packets on grill over hot coals, cook for 10 minutes, turn and cook for 10 minutes; check for doneness and cook additional minutes if necessary.

Yield: 4 servings

John and Denise Phillips
Fairfield, Alabama

Lemon Butter Dilled Fish

Bea Baab shares the source of the lemon butter:

"I learned about brown butter from reading a Rex Stout mystery."

2	pounds hybrid bass, striper or other white fish fillets, cut in serving-sized pieces
½	cup butter or margarine
1 to 2	tablespoons lemon juice
	Dill weed

Melt butter in small saucepan over medium heat; cook until lightly browned. Stir in lemon juice and pour into baking dish or pan large enough to contain a single layer of fish (tails overlapping) which has been greased or prepared with vegetable spray. Arrange in pan, overlapping thinner tails for equal thickness of fish. Sprinkle with dillweed. Bake at 350 degrees for 15 to 20 minutes or until fish is opaque.

To prepare on outdoor grill, place fish in pan shaped from aluminum foil; cover grill and cook over hot coals until done. Smoke gives added flavor to fish.

Yield: 4 servings

Bea Baab
Augusta, Georgia

Baked Shad

1	(5 to 8 pound) whole fresh shad, cleaned but skin intact

Place fish on heavy-duty aluminum foil rectangle; bring opposite edges together and fold to seal tightly. Place on baking sheet. Bake at 225 degrees for 6 to 8 hours. Serve warm.

The slow cooking method decalcifies bones, allowing them to be eaten easily.

James C. Wright, MD
Virginia Beach, Virginia

Fish Fillets with Tarragon

1 or 2	cloves garlic, minced
4 to 6	green onions, minced
2 or 3	sprigs parsley, minced
1	tablespoon minced tarragon leaves
¼	cup butter
4 to 6	flounder, sea trout, striper, largemouth bass or any non-oil white fish fillets
	Salt and black pepper to taste
	Juice of 1 lemon

Simmer garlic, onion, parsley and tarragon in butter for 1 to 2 minutes; do not brown. Season fillets with salt and pepper. Saute fillets in butter mixture for 2 to 4 minutes on each side, depending on thickness; do not overcook. Transfer fillets to warm serving dish. Remove butter mixture from stove and cool for 1 minute, stir in lemon juice and reheat briefly (do not boil). Pour over fillets. Add extra tarragon or garlic, if desired.

Yield: 3 or 4 servings

Jim Dean
Raleigh, North Carolina

Grilled Fish Fillets

½	cup vegetable oil
¼	cup lemon juice
½	teaspoon Worcestershire sauce
	Dash hot pepper sauce
2	teaspoons salt
¼	teaspoon white pepper
2	pounds freshwater fillets, cut in serving-sized pieces
	Dash paprika

Prepare grill to produce moderately hot coals. Combine oil, juice, sauces, salt and pepper. Place fish on well-greased grill 4 inches above coals. Baste with sauce and sprinkle with paprika. Cook for 8 minutes, baste and season again, turn and cook for 7 to 10 minutes or until fish flakes easily when probed with fork.

Yield: 4 to 6 servings

John and Denise Phillips
Fairfield, Alabama

Northern Fried Fish

1	egg, beaten
¼	cup milk
½	cup butter or margarine, divided
½	cup olive oil, divided
2	pounds hybrid bass, striper, or other white fish fillets, cut in serving-sized pieces
1	cup all-purpose flour

Beat egg and milk together in medium-sized bowl. Heat 2 tablespoons butter and 2 tablespoons olive oil in large skillet over medium heat. Dip each fillet into flour, then egg mixture and again in flour; place in skillet, adding fillets until bottom is covered but not crowded. Cook for 3 to 5 minutes until bottom is golden brown. Turn and fry on second side, adding more butter and oil as necessary. Place cooked fillets on paper towels on warm platter; fillets should be crunchy on the outside and moist on the inside. If pan drippings become too brown, clean the skillet and use fresh butter and oil.

Fried fish is especially good with boiled potatoes, green beans and a tossed salad. Extra fish can be used to make Fish Salad (page 147).

Yield: 4 servings

Bea Baab
Augusta, Georgia

Fillet with Mustard Marinade

Prepared mustard
Hot pepper sauce
Minced garlic
Salt
Black pepper
Bass, catfish or other fish fillets
Cornmeal
Vegetable oil

Combine seasonings in a plastic storage bag, mixing to form marinade. Add fillets and marinate for up to 4 hours. Drain fillets, dredge in cornmeal and deep fry in hot oil until golden brown.

Callie C. Spiller Jr.
Greensboro, North Carolina

Mustard Fried Fish

1   (16 ounce) carton sour cream
1   cup prepared mustard
    Whole bream, cleaned and scaled, or catfish
    fillets
    Cornmeal
    Salt and black pepper to taste
    Vegetable oil

Combine sour cream and mustard. Coat fish or fillets with mixture and let stand for 20 minutes. Season cornmeal with salt and pepper. Dredge fish in cornmeal mixture and deep fry in hot oil until browned.

Ronnie Strickland
Natchez, Mississippi

Spicy Fish Dip

1   cup mayonnaise or mayonnaise-type salad
    dressing
¾   cup Italian salad dressing
½   cup sour cream
3   tablespoons Dijon mustard
1   pound fish fillets, broiled and flaked

Combine mayonnaise, salad dressing, sour cream and mustard; mix thoroughly. Fold in flaked fish. Chill overnight to blend flavors. Serve with chips, crackers or fresh vegetables or as spread on toasted party breads.

Yield: 2½ cups

Howard P. Lindsey
Bowling Green, Kentucky

Fish Chowder

1 to 1½	pounds fresh or saltwater fish
	Water
¼	cup vinegar
6 to 8	peppercorns
1	cup diced ham or bacon
¼	cup butter
1	cup diced onion
1	cup diced celery
1	cup diced potatoes
2	(10¾ ounce) cans cream of celery soup, undiluted
	Milk
	Salt and black pepper to taste
	Hot pepper sauce (optional)

Poach fish in water with vinegar and peppercorns until fish flakes easily when probed with fork. Remove from water, drain and flake. Saute ham in butter for a few minutes, add vegetables and saute until vegetables are translucent, adding small amount of water if necessary to prevent scorching. Stir in soup and add milk to preferred consistency. Cook until very hot but do not allow to boil. Add fish and cook for a few more minutes over medium heat, stirring. Serve hot or cold.

Yield: 5 or 6 servings

Theo Titus III
Thomasville, Georgia

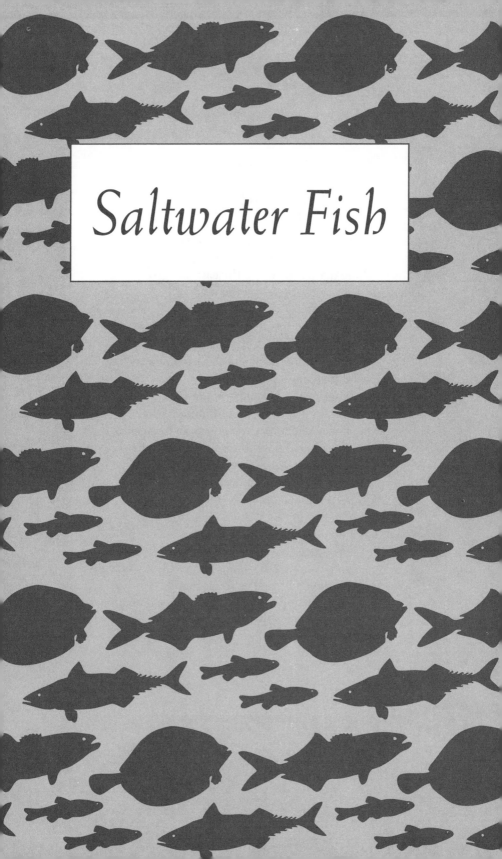

Saltwater Fish

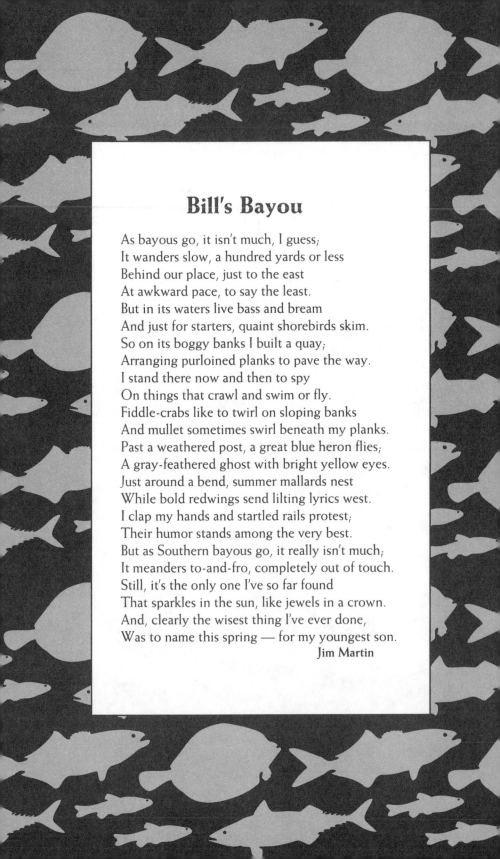

Bill's Bayou

As bayous go, it isn't much, I guess;
It wanders slow, a hundred yards or less
Behind our place, just to the east
At awkward pace, to say the least.
But in its waters live bass and bream
And just for starters, quaint shorebirds skim.
So on its boggy banks I built a quay;
Arranging purloined planks to pave the way.
I stand there now and then to spy
On things that crawl and swim or fly.
Fiddle-crabs like to twirl on sloping banks
And mullet sometimes swirl beneath my planks.
Past a weathered post, a great blue heron flies;
A gray-feathered ghost with bright yellow eyes.
Just around a bend, summer mallards nest
While bold redwings send lilting lyrics west.
I clap my hands and startled rails protest;
Their humor stands among the very best.
But as Southern bayous go, it really isn't much;
It meanders to-and-fro, completely out of touch.
Still, it's the only one I've so far found
That sparkles in the sun, like jewels in a crown.
And, clearly the wisest thing I've ever done,
Was to name this spring — for my youngest son.

                                    Jim Martin

Louisiana SEOPA Member Jailed During Fishing Tournament!

This is not a fish story. It all started off innocently enough. I was fishing a speckled trout tournament as a guest with a group of rank amateur speckled trout anglers. I fish for giant spotted sea trout with live bait and I use waders to walk around the shallow reefs of the Louisiana coast where the giants feed.

Using seventeen pound test line and a number four treble hook I picked out a live, giant croaker and hooked it right behind the eye and forward of the gills. I made the perfect cast near the shallow reefs in waist deep water.

The live croaker didn't stand a chance as a sea gull swooped down and picked up my bait. The gull gained altitude and when it was about six feet out of the water a giant silver, speckled form rose out of the water and grabbed the sea gull by the feet. Falling back into the water, bait, sea gull and fish started cutting waves towards the deep water of the Gulf of Mexico.

Before I could hit the release on my reel harness the line ran out and I felt my 225 pounds jerked into the water with a tremendous force. I was pulled across the top of the water with such speed my waders were turned inside out and peeled off of my body. With my body still hooked to the fishing harness and the harness to the reel I was helpless.

Anglers in a nearby boat saw that I was in trouble and cut their anchor rope in order to save time. Their two 200hp outboards roared to life and the boat at full throttle just managed to catch me.

While two men pulled me aboard, a third raised a high powered rifle with a scope and aiming at a point below the water line where the sea gull was thrashing, the man fired. The bullet shot the fish through both eyes and it stopped dead in the water.

As we pulled the fish into the boat everyone realized that it was a new Louisiana state and possibly a new world record. We iced the monster and put a towel over the angry, confused sea gull then headed for the beach and the weigh-in station.

A strange boat had been observing us and followed us to the weigh station. Once we landed we caused quite a bit of excitement. The sea gull had the barb from one of the hooks stuck through the web of its left foot and the second barb of the treble hook held the monster speckled trout.

Someone volunteered to remove the sea gull from the hook and that is when I realized that the boat that followed us from the reefs had contained a federal and a state wildlife agent. They were now assisting one another with the hook removal from the gull's foot.

The fish hit the scales at an unbelievable twenty-one pounds. Before I could become excited a protest arose from some members of the fishing club. They said that fishing with a live sea gull as bait was against club rules and there was a suspicious bulge in the stomach of the fish that had to be investigated.

Before I could blink one of the members of the club announced that he was a surgeon and had the fish opened up like a newspaper. The bulge turned out to be an eight pound speckled trout and the fishing club members accused me of stuffing the larger speckled trout with the eight pound fish for the prize money which was over $1,000.00. Cheating in a fishing tournament for that amount of money is a felony. One club member happened to be a deputy sheriff and he arrested me on the spot. The wildlife agents charged me with using a federally protected bird as fishing bait and once I got to jail the SPCA charged me with cruelty to animals.

My family was so embarrassed they refused to post bail and I think they left town. I am innocent but I need a good lawyer. Know any?

Edwin A. Vice
Lafayette, Louisiana

Sea Bass Tempura

1	cup whole wheat flour
1	teaspoon cornstarch
¼	teaspoon noniodized salt
1¼	cups cold water
2	pounds sea bass, skin removed, boned and cubed
	Sesame oil
	Vegetable flowerets and chunks

Combine flour, cornstarch and salt; add water and mix slowly until smooth. Batter must be cold to prevent oil absorption. Dip fish cubes into batter and deep fry in 2 inches oil heated to 370 degrees, cooking until golden brown. Dip vegetables in batter and fry.

James C. Wright, MD
Virginia Beach, Virginia

Striped Bass

2	(16 ounce) packages seasoned stuffing mix
1	(10 pound) striped bass (also known as Virginia Rockfish), cleaned and scaled
6	large potatoes
10 to 12	small onions
10	small carrots

Prepare stuffing mix according to package directions. Spoon mixture into cavity of fish; place in roasting pan or plastic cooking bag. Add vegetables around fish. Bake at 325 degrees for 1 hour; fish should flake when probed with fork. Bake for additional 15 to 20 minutes if necessary. Serve hot. Leftover fish can be saved and served cold the following day with mayonnaise spread, a mixture of ½ cup mayonnaise, ½ teaspoon thyme and the juice of 1 lemon.

Yield: 4 servings

James C. Wright, MD
Virginia Beach, Virginia

Broiled Bluefish

Dr. Jim uses spearmint and peppermint that "grow in my yard like weeds" for garnish with this bluefish.

1 to 2	pounds bluefish fillets
	Dijon mustard
	Mayonnaise
	Freshly grated Parmesan cheese
	Parsley sprigs for garnish

Place fillets, skin side down, on foil-covered baking sheet. Spread half the fillets with thin layer of mustard; cover other fillets with mayonnaise and sprinkle generously with cheese. Broil, 5 inches below heat source, until fish flakes when probed with fork, usually less than 10 minutes. Do not overcook. Garnish with parsley.

Yield: 4 servings

James C. Wright, MD
Virginia Beach, Virginia

Smoked Bluefish

4	(6 pound or larger) bluefish, filleted
1	gallon water
½	pound noniodized salt
1	(16 ounce) package dark brown sugar

Place fish in brine made by combining water, salt and sugar; let stand overnight. Remove fillets. Dry until a glaze appears, using an electric fan if necessary; drying may take 8 hours. Fillets must feel dry to the touch or smoked fish will be soggy. Prepare commercial smoker or charcoal grill, setting at low heat (120 degrees). Soak hickory or fruitwood chips in water and add to coals. If charcoal is used, cover most of coals with aluminum foil to avoid flame up. Place fillets on grill, skin side down. Smoke until meat is reduced in size and is chestnut color or darker; cooking time will vary with thickness of fillets but will average 2 to 4 hours. In temperature controlled cooker, 4 hours at 120 degrees plus 2 hours at 180 degrees works well.

This process relies on heat rather than cold smoking used for Smithfield hams. The fish is not preserved by salt but may be stored in plastic bags in the refrigerator for several weeks.

James C. Wright, MD
Virginia Beach, Virginia

Bluefish Salad

1 (6 pound or larger) bluefish, filleted
  Seafood seasoning
  Water
  Lettuce
  Seafood cocktail sauce

Remove skin and all dark meat from fillet. Cover generously with seafood seasoning and place in shallow baking dish. Chill for 1 hour. Cut fillet into small chunks. Boil chunks in water until fish flakes easily when probed with fork. Drain and discard liquid. Sprinkle more seaoning on chunks and chill until cold. Place lettuce leaves on serving plates, add layer of shredded lettuce and top with crumbled fish. Add cocktail sauce to taste.

Bluefish prepared this way tastes more like crab than bluefish.

James C. Wright, MD
Virginia Beach, Virginia

Fish Salad

Bea Baab recalls that when she was a child, her mother bought lobster bodies from the local lobster pound for 10 cents a dozen. The family would spend the evening cleaning "every little bit of meat" from the lobster, to be mixed with the celery and a dressing similar to Catalina and enjoyed the next day.

2 cups fried fish chunks
½ cup chopped celery
½ cup Catalina salad dressing
  Lettuce leaves
  Mayonnaise

Combine fish, broken into small pieces, with celery and dressing. Chill, covered, overnight. Stir once or twice, adding more dressing if necessary to keep it moist. Serve on lettuce with a dollop of mayonnaise. If desired, serve with carrot, celery, cucumber and bell pepper sticks, tomato wedges, ripe olives, sweet pickles, Cheddar and Swiss cheese sticks and hard-cooked egg quarters.

Yield: 4 servings

Bea Baab
Augusta, Georgia

Amberjack a la Chef Andy

Dr. Jim claims that Chef Andy freely gives him recipes "because I never will take the time to prepare them his way." He has tried this amberjack recipe and suggests that the finished product is the reason Chef Andy is considered a gourmet.

4	(½-inch thick) amberjack steaks, cleaned and skin removed
1	cup vegetable oil (not olive)
	Juice of 1 lemon
	Pinch of noniodized salt
	Pinch of freshly ground black pepper
1	tablespoon dill weed
½	cup plus 1 tablespoon white vinegar, divided
1	cup white wine
½	cup chopped onion
1 ½	cups whipping cream (not half and half)
2	tablespoons roux
2	tablespoons chopped tarragon
2	tablespoons chopped basil
2	tablespoons chopped dill
2	tablespoons chopped garlic
	Salt and black pepper to taste
	Steamed vegetables of choice

Combine oil, lemon juice, noniodized salt, fresh pepper, dill weed and 5 tablespoons vinegar. Place steaks in marinade and chill overnight. Before cooking steaks, prepare sauce by combining wine, ¼ cup vinegar and onion in saucepan; cook until moisture is evaporated, then add cream, roux made from flour and butter, and seasonings. Bring to a steady simmer; blend until smooth. In skillet lightly brushed with olive oil, grill steaks for 3 minutes on each side. Place on dinner plates, add steamed vegetables and pour sauce mix over steaks and vegetables.

Yield: 4 servings

James C. Wright, MD
Virginia Beach, Virginia

"Things usually work out for the best on fishing trips, especially if you aren't the one who lost the big fish."

Charley Dickey

Puppy Drum

1   (3 to 5 pound) puppy drum, dressed but skin
    intact
4   large or 8 small potatoes, unpeeled
8   carrots
8   small onions

Place fish and vegetables on large heavy-duty aluminum foil rectangle. Fold edges of foil together to form tightly sealed packet. Bake at 350 degrees for 1 hour.

Yield: 4 servings

James C. Wright, MD
Virginia Beach, Virginia

Broiled Flounder

1   pound flounder fillets
    Italian salad dressing
    Butter, softened
    Lemon juice
    Lemon slices, paprika and parsley sprigs for
    garnish

Marinate fillets in salad dressing for several hours. Place fillets, skin side down, on aluminum foil covered baking sheet. Lightly spread butter on top of fillets. Broil for about 10 minutes or until lightly browned. Garnish with lemon slices, paprika and parsley sprigs.

Flounder is low in fat but does not have distinctive flavor unless fat (salad dressing and butter in this recipe) is added. A low-calorie alternative is to cook non-marinated flounder in a microwave oven and season with salt, pepper and lemon juice.

Yield: 2 or 3 servings

James C. Wright, MD
Virginia Beach, Virginia

Flounder Fancy Rollups

⅓   cup margarine or butter
⅓   cup fresh lemon juice
2   chicken-flavored bouillon cubes
1   teaspoon hot pepper sauce
1   cup cooked white rice
1   (10 ounce) package frozen chopped broccoli, thawed
1   cup (4 ounces) shredded sharp Cheddar cheese
2   pounds flounder fillets
    Paprika or parsley sprigs for garnish

Melt margarine in small saucepan; add lemon juice, bouillon cubes and hot pepper sauce. Combine rice, broccoli and cheese; add half the lemon butter and mix well. Place fillets, skin side down, on work surface. Spoon equal portions of broccoli mixture on each fillet and roll up; place in shallow baking dish. Pour remaining lemon butter over rollups. Bake at 375 degrees for 25 minutes. Garnish with paprika or parsley sprigs.

Yield: 4 servings

James C. Wright, MD
Virginia Beach, Virginia

Haddock Stew

1   onion, chopped
    Olive oil
1   (29 ounce) can tomatoes
1   teaspoon chopped parsley
    Salt and black pepper to taste
    Oregano to taste
3   potatoes, cut in chunks
2   pounds haddock fillets

Saute onion in small amount of oil in large saucepan. Add tomatoes and seasonings. Simmer for 30 minutes. Add potatoes and cook until partially tender. Add fish and cook until it flakes when probed with fork. Serve as stew or as sauce over spaghetti.

Yield: 4 servings

Camella Garitta
East Haven, Connecticut

Halibut

2   pounds halibut
1   clove garlic, crushed
½   cup vegetable oil
2   cups (8 ounces) shredded mozzarella cheese
     Italian seasoned breadcrumbs

Cut fish into 1x½x4-inch strips. Stir garlic into oil in shallow bowl. Dip fish strips into oil to coat on all sides but do not soak. Place on aluminum-foil covered baking sheet, arranging in groups of 4 with edges just touching. Sprinkle cheese on strips and top with generous sprinkling of breadcrumbs. Broil, 5 inches below the heat source, for about 10 minutes; avoid overbrowning. Leftover fish can be reheated in microwave oven.

Yield: 4 to 6 servings

James C. Wright, MD
Virginia Beach, Virginia

Grilled Atlantic Mackeral

8   Atlantic mackeral fillets
     Salt and black pepper to taste

Place fillets, skin side down, over medium heat of outdoor grill. Season with salt and pepper. Grill until fish flakes when probed with fork, usually in 10 minutes or less.

Yield: 4 servings

James C. Wright, MD
Virginia Beach, Virginia

Salted Atlantic Mackeral

10 pounds coarse noniodized salt
50 Atlantic mackeral fillets (or more)
1 cup white cider vinegar

Pour layer of salt in bottom of clean 5-gallon plastic bucket. Arrange a single layer of fillets, skin side down, on salt. Add layer of salt, then another layer of fillets but with skin side up. Alternately add layers of salt and fillets until all fillets are used. Store in cool area. Self-brine will form in a few days; use weighted plate to hold top layer under brine surface. Add vinegar to retain white fillet color. To use, soak 1 or 2 fillets per person overnight in tap water. Boil and serve for breakfast.

Salted fish will keep for 6 to 12 months. Because mackeral is oily, do not freeze. Salted mackeral should be avoided by persons on a low-sodium diet and have a high calorie content.

Yield: 25 servings

James C. Wright, MD
Virginia Beach, Virginia

Smoked Atlantic Mackeral

½ pound salt
1 (16 ounce) package brown sugar
1 gallon water
20 to 30 Atlantic mackeral fillets

Dissolve salt and sugar in water in 5-gallon plastic bucket; do not use metal container. Soak fillets for 1 to 2 hours in brine. Dry fillets, blotting until glaze appears. Prepare covered grill or commercial smoker with low heat. Place wet hickory on fruitwood (apple, cherry or peach) chips. Place aluminum foil over heat and smoke source to avoid flame up. Place fillets, skin side down, on grill. Cook for 1 to 2 hours over low heat producing plenty of smoke; fillets should be medium brown or darker. If fillets dry out, heat is too high in smoker.

Yield: 10 to 15 servings

James C. Wright, MD
Virginia Beach, Virginia

Baked King Mackeral

When the kings are running, Ginnie Jennewein prefers this stuffed version. A martini, while the fish is baking, makes it a delightful meal but isn't necessary for the full enjoyment of the fish—just to liven up the guests.

> Bread stuffing
> Chopped onion
> Chopped celery
> Salt and black pepper to taste
> Tarragon to taste
> 1 (10 to 20 pound) king mackeral, cleaned and head removed
> Bacon slices

Prepare bread stuffing, using onion, celery and seasonings to taste, in quantity sufficient to fill fish cavity. Spoon stuffing into cavity and secure edges with wooden picks or skewers. Place fish on rack in large broiling pan. Cover fish with bacon slices. Bake at 375 degrees until done, checking by separating flesh at thickest part; meat should be opaque through to the bone. Serve hot in slices or chunks.

Yield: 8 servings

Paul Jennewein
Wrightsville Beach, North Carolina

Grilled Spanish Mackeral

Dr. Jim considers these "about the tastiest fish in the ocean when eaten the same day they were caught" but never bothers to freeze them because of the high fat content.

> 8 Spanish mackeral fillets, skin intact
> Salt and black pepper to taste

Place fillets, skin side down, on grill surface, 5 inches above heat source. Cover with grill lid. Cook until fillets flake easily when probed with fork, usually 5 to 7 minutes. Season with salt and pepper.

Yield: 4 servings

James C. Wright, MD
Virginia Beach, Virginia

Spanish Mackeral in Foil

1   large Spanish onion, thickly sliced
8   Spanish mackeral fillets, skin intact
     Zucchini strips
     Carrot strips, cooked
     Red bell pepper strips
     Yellow bell pepper strips
     Salt and black pepper to taste
     Paprika or pink peppercorns

Place onion slices on 4 large heavy-duty aluminum foil rectangles. Arrange 2 fillets, skin side down, side by side to form rectangle on onion. Place vegetable strips beside fillets. Sprinkle with seasonings. Bring opposite edges of foil together and roll to form tightly sealed packet. Place packets on grill, seam side up, and cook over medium heat. Fillets will be done when steam inflates aluminum packets, usually 8 to 10 minutes. Do not open packet until ready to serve.

All types of fresh vegetables may be cooked with fillets.

Yield: 4 servings

Bruce Wright, MD
Virginia Beach, Virginia

Quick Spanish Mackeral

8   Spanish mackeral fillets
     Salt and black pepper to taste
     Butter (optional)

Place fillets, skin side down, on microwave-safe plate. Season with salt and pepper. Add pat of butter. Microwave, covered, at high setting for 2½ to 3 minutes; do not overcook.

Butter may be omitted but it prevents formation of unattractive liquid scum on fish surface.

Yield: 4 servings

Bruce Wright, MD
Virginia Beach, Virginia

Salmon Mousse

1	envelope unflavored gelatin
¼	cup warm water
½	cup chicken broth
1	tablespoon chopped dill
½	cup mayonnaise
1	tablespoon lemon juice
2	small green onions, chopped
½	teaspoon paprika
1	teaspoon noniodized salt
2	cups flaked cooked salmon
1	cup whipping cream (not half and half)
	Dill sprigs
	Assorted crackers

Dissolve gelatin in warm water in large mixing bowl. Stir in broth. Add dill and let stand for 10 to 15 minutes. Add mayonnaise, lemon juice, onion, paprika and salt; mix thoroughly. Chill until partially thickened, usually about 30 minutes. Stir in salmon and mix well. Whip cream until stiff. Fold whipped cream into salmon mixture. Pour into oiled 1½ to 2-quart fish-shaped mold. Chill several hours or until firm. To serve, invert on plate and shake to loosen. Garnish with dill sprigs and serve with assorted crackers.

Yield: 6 cups

James C. Wright, MD
Virginia Beach, Virginia

"He…dug out a tattered magazine clipping. I could just make out the words: 'Allah does not deduct from the allotted time of man those hours spent in fishing.'"

Charlie Elliott

Shark Shisk Kebab

2	pounds spiny dogfish (shark) fillets, cut in 1-inch cubes
	Vinegar
	Water
¼	cup soy sauce
3	tablespoons lemon juice
½	cup vegetable oil
1	cup pineapple juice
12 to 18	whole mushrooms
12	cherry tomatoes
3	small onions, quartered
3	large green bell peppers, cut in large chunks
1	(8 ounce) can pineapple chunks

Soak fish cubes in vinegar and water solution for about 1 hour to remove odor. Drain, then marinate cubes in mixture of soy sauce, lemon juice, oil and pineapple juice, storing in refrigerator. Prepare charcoal grill to produce medium heat. Alternate vegetables and pineapple with fish cubes on skewers. Grill, turning and basting occasionally, for 15 minutes.

Spiny dogfish should be cleaned immediately after it's caught. Fillet each side, remove skin, rinse and place in plastic bag on ice until ready to use.

Yield: 6 servings

James C. Wright, MD
Virginia Beach, Virginia

"Have you ever fished at night on the Southern coast when the moon was down? Every ripple, every splash, is like the wash of phosphorescent quicksilver across transparent velvet."

Charlie Elliott

Barbecued Tautog

2   pounds tautog steaks
½   cup ketchup
¼   cup vegetable oil
3   tablespoons lemon juice
2   tablespoons cider vinegar
1   teaspoon Worcestershire sauce
½   teaspoon grated onion
1   clove garlic, crushed
½   teaspoon noniodized salt
½   teaspoon dry mustard
¼   teaspoon paprika

Place steaks in plastic bag with zip closure. Add ketchup, oil, lemon juice, vinegar, Worcestershire sauce, onion, garlic and seasonings to steaks. Chill for 30 minutes, occasionally turning to coat steaks with marinade on all sides. Prepare charcoal or propane grill to produce medium heat. Grill fillets, basting with marinade, for 8 to 10 minutes, turn, and grill for 8 to 10 minutes; fish should flake when probed with fork.

Commercial barbecue sauce may be substituted for marinade.

Yield: 4 servings

James C. Wright, MD
Virginia Beach, Virginia

Fish Chowder

1	pound tautog fillets
2	cups water
1	bay leaf
¼	teaspoon black pepper
1	medium-sized onion, chopped
¼	cup butter
¼	cup all-purpose flour
2½	cups evaporated milk
1½	cups fish broth
¼	teaspoon dried thyme
¼	teaspoon dried oregano
1	teaspoon parsley flakes
1	cup (4 ounces) grated Monterey Jack or Muenster cheese
	Salt and black pepper to taste

Combine fillets, water, bay leaf and ¼ teaspoon pepper in saucepan. Simmer, covered, until fish flakes easily when probed with fork. Remove from heat, remove fish and reserve 1½ cups broth. Saute onion in butter until tender. Stir in flour and mix thoroughly. Add milk, stirring constantly. Stir in broth. Add flaked fish, seasonings and cheese. Simmer for at least 15 minutes. Season with salt and pepper.

Yield: 4 servings

James C. Wright, MD
Virginia Beach, Virginia

"I have never understood why fishermen are so afraid to come right out and admit they got clobbered. It is the nature of any sport that sometimes you win and other times you lose. We all understand it."

Charley Dickey

Triggerfish

Despite an appetite for almost any bait that drops near him in the deep waters of the Gulf or Atlantic Ocean off the Florida coast, the triggerfish can be a delicious dinner if properly handled. Triggerfish hide is almost as tough and rough as the garfish that American Indians used to cover their war shields.

To clean and dress triggerfish, get to the fine grain white meat tenderloin on each side of the backbone by using a sharp knife to puncture the skin. Cut until the blade stops on the rib cage. The 30 per cent of the garfish that is usable lies in the two tenderloins along the back; the belly and rib meat is too difficult to separate from the bones to be practical for food.

Jerk the tough skin off with pliers or similar tool. The two resulting fillets will vary in size from 4 to 6 inches long by 1 inch deep and 1 inch wide.

To fry, season the tenderloins with salt and pepper, dredge in cornmeal and drop into hot deep fat to fry to a golden brown. In a few minutes, they resemble fried chicken nuggets and taste much better.

To broil, season with salt and pepper and baste with lemon juice or butter as they cook slowly over charcoal or a gas flame.

To boil, cut the fillets into nugget chunks, cook in boiling water for 2 to 3 minutes, remove and dip into butter or lemon juice. The taste is much like lobster or scallops.

To make chowder, use triggerfish with the same ingredients as used in a clam chowder. The fish cooks quickly.

W. Horace Carter
Hawthorne, Florida

Tuna

½   pound fresh tuna, not fake albacore or little tuny

1   can powdered wasahi (Japanese horseradish)
Low-sodium teriyaki sauce

Immediately after tuna is caught, cut gill plate to bleed it; ice down. Mix small amount of wasahi with teriyaki sauce in 1:5 proportion; stir well and let stand a few minutes. Cut thin slices, ⅟₁₆-inch thick and size of postage stamp, of cold fresh tuna. Dip tuna in wasahi mixture. Eat immediately.

Some authorities recommend against eating raw fish in any form.

James C. Wright, MD
Virginia Beach, Virginia

Grilled Tuna Steaks

4   (½ to 1-inch thick) slices tuna
Soy sauce

Marinate tuna in soy sauce in shallow baking dish for 1 hour in refrigerator, turning occasionally. Prepare outdoor grill to produce medium heat. Basting with soy sauce occasionally, grill tuna, turning once, for about 20 minutes.

Yellowfin tuna has a lower fat content and slightly lower calorie count than bluefin tuna.

Yield: 4 servings

James C. Wright, MD
Virginia Beach, Virginia

Canned Tuna

Fresh tuna
Noniodized salt
Vegetable oil

Keep freshly caught fish cool but do not soak in ice water. Trim and discard red meat; cut remaining fish into 1-inch chunks. Pack chunks into sterilized wide-mouth pint jars, filling to ½ inch below rim. Add ½ teaspoon salt and 1 teaspoon oil to each jar; add tap water to ½ inch below rim. Remove trapped air by sliding table knife in and around chunks; refill to ½ inch below rim. Apply lids, screwing on tightly. Process in pressure cooker at 10 pounds pressure for 1 hour and 5 minutes or in water bath cooker at gentle boil for 3 hours and 5 minutes.

Canned tuna is good for dozens of years; frozen tuna lasts just a couple of months.

James C. Wright, MD
Virginia Beach, Virginia

Blackened Fish

While Chef Paul Prudhomme is generally given credit for popularizing blackened redfish, Dr. Jim believes the chef, as a youth, must have been exposed to Mother Wright's cooking. "She invented blackened fish to go along with her blackened chicken, blackened fried potatoes and several other items," Dr. Jim recalls. "I learned to enjoy it before I ever ate it in a restaurant."

4   (8 ounce, ½ to 1-inch thick) cobia, amberjack, drum, tuna, shark or swordfish steaks
       Italian salad dressing
       Vegetable oil

Place cast iron skillet on grill; do not add oil until the skillet is white hot. Marinate steaks in salad dressing. Drain steak, then place in skillet; be wary of hot steam it produces. First side usually blackens in 30 seconds, turn, and second side usually cooks in 1 minute. If heat diminishes, cooking will take longer. Additional steaks usually take somewhat longer cooking time.

Yield: 4 servings

James C. Wright, MD
Virginia Beach, Virginia

Ceviche

Frozen triggerfish or sheepshead fillets, thawed
and diced
Onion, diced
Tomatoes, diced
Minced fresh parsley
Extra-virgin olive oil
Balsamic vinegar
Lime juice
Salt and black pepper to taste
Crackers

Combine equal parts fish, onion and tomatoes; place in glass bowl. Sprinkle with parsley, a dash of oil and a dash of vinegar. Add lime juice to cover mixture. Chill, covered, overnight in refrigerator. Serve, seasoned with salt and pepper, with crackers the following day.

Because the fish is not cooked, safeguard against parasites by freezing any white fish intended for ceviche. Do not use unfrozen freshwater fish because of parasite potential.

Humberto Fontova
Covington, Louisiana

Marinated Fish

Fish fillets or steaks
⅓   cup Italian salad dressing
1   tablespoon liquid smoke

Marinate fish with salad dressing and liquid smoke in 1-gallon plastic bag with zip closure; chill overnight. Grill over coals.

If preparing a 30 to 40 pound fish, cut it into chunks, marinate overnight, dredge in breadcrumbs and fry instead of grilling. To grill extra tender fish such as trout, cut across the grain in ½ to 1-inch chunks to better maintain shape.

Colette Moreau Lottinger
Luling, Louisiana

Fish Fillet Pizzaiole

2   pounds fresh dolphin, southern grouper or northern cod or haddock fillets
2   cloves garlic, cut
1   (16 ounce) jar spaghetti sauce
1   (8 ounce) package mozarella cheese slices
    Paprika

Rub fillets with garlic and place on broiler pan. Broil fillets for 5 minutes per 1 inch thickness. Cut into 2x6-inch bars and return to broiler pan. Spoon spaghetti sauce on each bar, top with cheese and sprinkle with paprika. Broil for 3 minutes or until cheese is lightly browned.

Yield: 4 servings

Bob T. Epstein
Tavernier, Florida

Fish Sauce Piquante

1   teaspoon butter
6   white trout or other soft fish fillets
1   (11 ounce) jar medium spicy chunky salsa
    Hot cooked rice

Melt butter in skillet over medium-high heat. Add fillets and salsa. Cook, stirring to break fillets into pieces, until fish is done. Serve over rice.

Yield: 4 servings

Ann Taylor
Boutte, Louisiana

Seafood Marinade

1	cup vegetable oil
1	cup lemon juice
2	teaspoons Italian salad dressing mix
2	tablespoons soy sauce
¼	cup firmly-packed brown sugar
½	cup chopped green onion
2	teaspoons seasoned salt
	Dash blackened redfish or Cajun seasoning
	Minced garlic
	Freshly grated ginger

Combine all ingredients. Marinate seafood for 2 to 4 hours prior to grilling or broiling. Heat excess marinade, bringing to a boil, and use as sauce for grilling.

Yield: 2½ cups

Libby Jicha
Atlanta, Georgia

Sage Baste for Grilled Fish

1	tablespoon white wine vinegar
1½	tablespoons chopped fresh sage or 1 teaspoon dried sage
	Salt and black pepper to taste
¼	cup olive oil

Whisk vinegar and seasonings together. Gradually add oil in stream, whisking until emulsified. To use, brush fish with sauce and grill, sauced side down, on a well-oiled rack 5 to 6 inches above heat source; baste and turn once. Fish should flake easily when probed with fork.

Baste is excellent with grouper and other flaky white fish.

Yield: ⅓ cup

Libby Jicha
Atlanta, Georgia

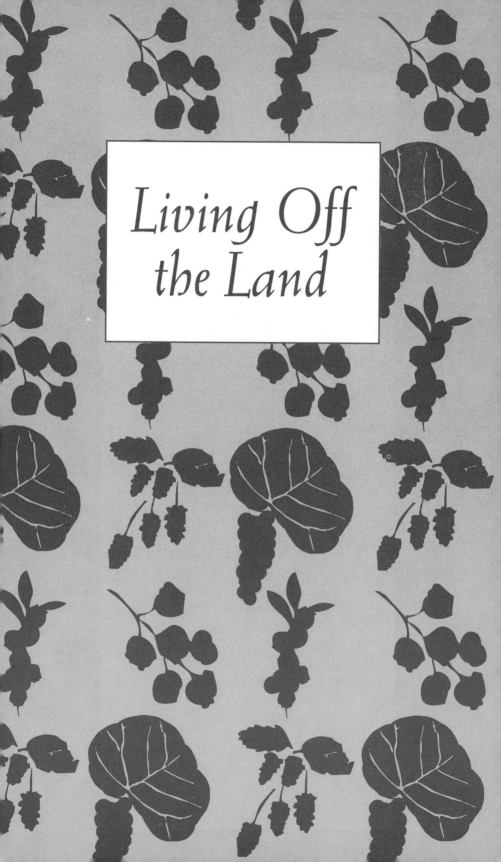

Living Off
the Land

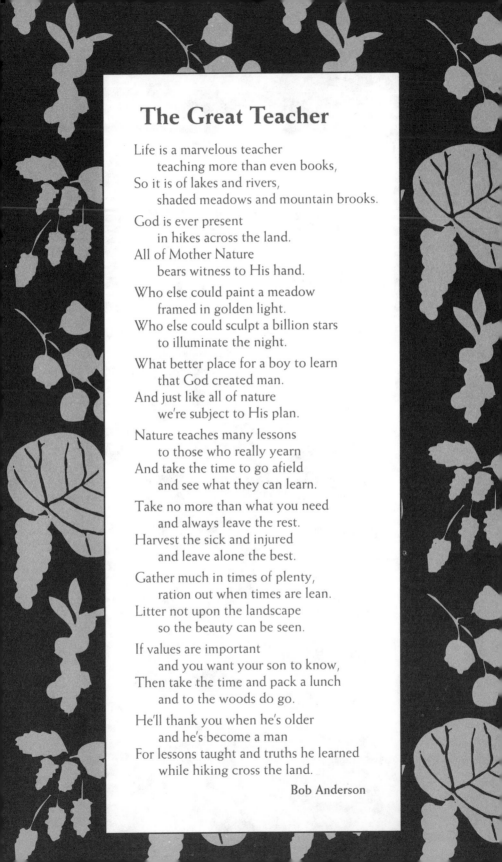

The Great Teacher

Life is a marvelous teacher
 teaching more than even books,
So it is of lakes and rivers,
 shaded meadows and mountain brooks.

God is ever present
 in hikes across the land.
All of Mother Nature
 bears witness to His hand.

Who else could paint a meadow
 framed in golden light.
Who else could sculpt a billion stars
 to illuminate the night.

What better place for a boy to learn
 that God created man.
And just like all of nature
 we're subject to His plan.

Nature teaches many lessons
 to those who really yearn
And take the time to go afield
 and see what they can learn.

Take no more than what you need
 and always leave the rest.
Harvest the sick and injured
 and leave alone the best.

Gather much in times of plenty,
 ration out when times are lean.
Litter not upon the landscape
 so the beauty can be seen.

If values are important
 and you want your son to know,
Then take the time and pack a lunch
 and to the woods do go.

He'll thank you when he's older
 and he's become a man
For lessons taught and truths he learned
 while hiking cross the land.

Bob Anderson

Pickin'

One of my fondest childhood memories centers on countless spring, summer and fall days spent plucking the fruits of nature's labor. Berrying and related pursuits gave me precious pocket money and provided the basic essentials for all sorts of tasty treats and days of glorious fun.

Of all these wild wonders, my personal favorite is the strawberry, a preference shared by Izaak Walton, who summed up its virtues nicely three centuries ago: "Doubtless God could have made a better berry, but doubtless God never did." Humankind has succeeded in producing a bigger berry but when it comes to taste, the wild strawberry has it all over its domesticated cousin. Adorning late-spring meadows and abandoned fields, these little red jewels could convince even Texans that bigger is not necessarily better.

By way of contrast, the next berry to make its annual ripening appearance is large but of distinctly humble origins. The child of farmed-out land and barren patches of red clay, this black beauty is often overlooked. Yet connoisseurs welcome his seasonal return with a joy born of past experience for they recognize the dewberry's true merits. Few poets have sung his praises but virtues he has, and in abundance. The glories of a dewberry cobbler are such that it may be just as well that relatively few have experienced them.

Dewberries are closely related to what is far and away the best-known of the wild brambles: the luscious, omnipresent blackberry. Old Will Shakespeare, who seemed to know something about everything, once wished that "reasons were as plentiful as blackberries." He was right on the mark. Botanists indicate that there are literally hundreds of subspecies of blackberries and anyone who has picked a pailful has likely noticed subtle variations in appearance and nature. In fact, genetic engineering has now produced a thornless blackberry, a row of which adorns the lower edge of my garden. However, no self-respecting berry picker feels that he has fulfilled all the requirements of his job until his hands are well-scratched, briar-riddled and stained a lovely purple-black hue. When it comes to blackberries, "no pain, no gain" is certainly the operative truism.

Happily, blackberries ripen at the same time as another widespread, plentiful fruit. This is the juicy, reddish-yellow wild plum. Old-timers, anticipating the ripe plums of high summer, mark the tree's whereabouts in early spring, when the warming sun covers the branches with lovely, aromatic blossoms. Plums plucked at their absolute ripest or gathered from the ground after their skin-bursting downfall, are a temptation which can lead the strongest of wills to overindulgence. They make marvelous jelly, rose-hued but clear, and are perhaps the most easily gathered of all wild fruits.

Another berry in great plentitude is the elderberry. Though without the thorny protection of most of its brethren, this particular berry is sadly neglected today. Once removed from the cluster of stems which hold them together, elderberries lend themselves to a variety of uses. They make a quite passable pie, toothsome jelly and a wine or cordial beyond compare. Indeed, for those inclined to sample an occasional alcoholic libation, raspberries, blackberries and elderberries, not to mention muscadines, each produce a delicate wine which, when properly made, is sheer nectar.

Once elderberries have come and gone, the best of the summer's berrying is past. Nonetheless, huckleberries and gooseberries remain, though their small size makes for tedious picking.

Fall brings rose hips, tasty and full of vitamin C, along with the many edible nuts, and two fruits of pure pleasure: muscadines and persimmons.

The dark purple muscadine grapes are delicious straight from the vine and make a jelly that is a first-rate accompaniment for game dishes as well as breads. And anyone who goes through life without putting a tooth to a country cook's muscadine pie is a deprived soul!

My grandmother used to maintain that only a fool would leave the persimmons to the raccoons, foxes, possums and deer. Anyone who has dug into the filling richness of a persimmon pudding is likely to agree. Similarly, persimmon butter livens a biscuit to a delightful degree. Incidentally, the myth that persimmons are no good until after a frost is just that—a myth. They normally reach full ripeness and begin to fall about the time of fall's first really cool spell. But be sure they are ripe, for a green persimmon's alum-like tartness can give an entirely new meaning to what teenagers refer to as "pucker power"!

Though winter's cold may post its "no berry picking" sign, nature's promise is of spring's renewing pleasure and mouthwatering dreams of delicacies to come—from pickin'!

Jim Casada
Rock Hill, South Carolina

Wild Berry Cobbler

1	cup all-purpose flour
1	cup sugar
2	teaspoons baking powder
1	cup milk
¼	cup butter, melted
2 to 4	cups fresh blackberries, dewberries, elderberries, huckleberries or strawberries

Combine flour, sugar, baking powder and milk; stir with wire whisk until smooth. Add melted butter and blend. Pour batter into 13x9x2-inch baking pan. Pour berries (amount depends on personal preference) evenly over batter. Bake at 350 degrees for 30 to 40 minutes or until golden brown.

Leftovers may be reheated in a microwave oven.

Yield: 6 to 8 servings

Jim and Ann Casada
Rock Hill, South Carolina

Fresh Berry Pie

1½	cups sugar
⅓	cup all-purpose flour
½	teaspoon cinnamon
4	cups fresh blackberries, blueberries, boysenberries, loganberries, raspberries, strawberries or other ripe juicy berries Pastry for 2-crust 9-inch pie
1½	tablespoons butter

Combine sugar, flour and cinnamon. Pour mixture over berries and mix lightly. Pour berries into pie pan lined with ½ of pastry. Dot with butter. Roll remaining pastry in circle to fit pan, place over berries and flute edges to enclose. Cover pastry edges with 1½-inch wide strip of aluminum foil to prevent excessive browning. Bake at 425 degrees for 35 to 45 minutes or until crust is golden brown and juice begins to bubble through crust. Serve warm but not hot.

Yield: 6 to 8 servings

John and Denise Phillips
Fairfield, Alabama

Easy as Pie Blackberry Cobbler

June is blackberry time in Mississippi. Jim McCafferty says there are plenty of them, there for the picking. Drive down any country road and look for them in fairly open areas, along the edges of woods, on ditchbanks, along fence rows, on recently cutover forest land and around old home sites. The mature fruit is deep blue-black, a cluster of pulp-covered seeds usually less than ¾ inch long. "The person who first coined 'mixed blessing' must have had the blackberry in mind," Jim says. "Though the fruit is plentiful and sweet, it's tough to harvest and the would-be berry pickers must be prepared to brave not only the thorns of the bush itself but the bites and stings of the chiggers, ticks and bees which make their homes or livings in the blackberry patch." To make it easier, Jim recommends looking for a large patch rather than sparse vines, delaying the picking if there are more red berries than ripe ones, picking early or late but not in the heat of the day, wearing a hat and carrying some water, bug protection, watching out for snakes, wearing long pants and a long-sleeved shirt, and washing the berries before eating.

2	cups blackberries
¾	cup sugar, divided
2	tablespoons water
¼	cup melted butter or margarine
¾	cup all-purpose flour
1	tablespoon baking powder
¼	teaspoon salt
½	cup milk or half and half
	Ice cream

Combine berries, ½ cup sugar and water in saucepan. Cook over medium heat until sugar is melted and berries are soft and syrup consistency. Spread butter in bottom of 1½-quart baking dish. Blend flour, baking powder, salt and milk; pour into baking dish but do not stir. Pour cooked berries over batter. Sprinkle ¼ cup sugar over berries. Bake at 400 degrees for 30 minutes. Serve with ice cream.

Yield: 4 to 6 servings

Jim McCafferty
Ridgeland, Mississippi

"If you want an hour of the purest, most wholesome enjoyment you can find, let those fleeting moments between daylight and sunrise in late spring find you in the woods or on a stream."

Charlie Elliott

Quick and Easy Blackberry Cobbler

8	cups blackberries
½	cup lemon juice
4	cups sugar
¼	cup butter
1	unbaked 9-inch pastry shell (optional)
2	(8 count) tubes refrigerated biscuits
	Whipped cream or ice cream

Mash berries. Combine berries, lemon juice, sugar and butter in saucepan. Bring to a boil, reduce heat and simmer for about 10 minutes or until berries change color and mixture is thickened. Pour into pastry shell or buttered 8-inch square baking dish. Arrange biscuits on top of hot berries and bake according to package directions or at 400 to 425 degrees for about 12 minutes. Serve hot with dollop of whipped cream or scoop of ice cream.

Yield: 6 to 8 servings

Tom Squier
Aberdeen, North Carolina

Blackberry Flying Saucers

| 2 | slices bread, buttered on all sides |
| 3 to 4 | tablespoons blackberry jam or ⅓ cup fresh blackberries sweetened with sugar or honey and sprinkled with cinnamon |

Using a clamp style cooker for making sealed sandwiches, place 1 slice bread in each side of cooker. Place jam or blackberries on bottom slice. Close cooker and heat over campfire or stove. Let cool for a few minutes before eating.

Yield: 1 serving

Marian Van Atta
Sapphire, North Carolina

Blackberry Leaf Tea

1   handful fresh green blackberry leaves
2   cups water
    Honey

Simmer leaves in water for 10 minutes. Strain into cups and sweeten with honey.

Yield: 2 servings

Marian Van Atta
Sapphire, North Carolina

Blueberry-Lemon Custard

John and Denise Phillips don't have blueberries in their own garden but enjoy picking at blueberry farms across the country while on camping trips. This recipe is manageable on a campstove with careful attention to the cooking of the custard.

4   eggs
⅓   cup sugar
⅛   teaspoon salt
1   cup milk
½   cup lemon juice
1   teaspoon grated lemon peel
3   cups blueberries

Beat eggs with sugar and salt; pour into top of double boiler over gently boiling water. Stir in milk and lemon juice; cook, stirring often, until thickened. Add lemon peel. Chill custard. Layer blueberries and custard in parfait glasses and chill until ready to serve.

If camping, spoon custard and berries into paper cups, cover with plastic wrap and chill in ice chest.

Yield: 8 servings

John and Denise Phillips
Fairfield, Alabama

Mulberry Leather

Marian Van Atta believes the mulberry has been "very underrated." She's picked black and red mulberries in Florida, red ones in Iowa and Missouri and white ones in British Columbia. Full ripe berries are delicious eaten out of hand and can be frozen with no additional sugar.

1	cup mulberry puree
⅓	cup sugar or honey
1	tablespoon lemon juice

Combine puree, made by blending berries, sweetening and lemon juice. Pour into oiled pan to form ¼-inch depth. Place in cold oven, set temperature to 300 degrees, and bake for 20 minutes. Turn oven off but leave leather in warm oven for 3 to 4 hours or until fruit will lift from the pan in thin sheets.

Marian Van Atta
Sapphire, North Carolina

Mulberry Shortcake

4	cups mulberries
1	cup honey or sugar
	Cinnamon
	Nutmeg
1	egg, beaten
½	cup milk
¼	cup vegetable oil
2	tablespoons honey or brown sugar
1½	cups all-purpose flour
1	tablespoon baking powder
½	teaspoon salt

Pour mulberries into greased 12x8x2-inch baking dish. Pour honey or sugar over berries. Sprinkle with cinnamon and nutmeg. Combine egg, milk, oil and honey or brown sugar in mixing bowl; blend well. Fold in flour, baking powder and salt, adding a small amount of milk if necessary to form very soft dough. Spread dough over berries. Bake at 400 degrees for about 20 minutes or until wooden pick comes out clean.

Yield: 6 to 8 servings

Tom Squier
Aberdeen, North Carolina

Seagrape Tapioca

When Marian Van Atta taught at the Florida Institute of Technology in Melbourne, she found seagrape plants growing next to her classroom. And when doing a radio show in Orlando, Florida, she discovered a clump of seagrapes, full of ripe fruit, growing at a shopping center. Because the fruit, which grows in bunches like other grapes, ripens just a few at a time, she places a bucket beneath the bunches and runs her fingers through the fruit, dislodging the ripe ones and leaving the immature.

2½	cups seagrape juice
½	cup sugar
¼	cup tapioca
	Juice of 1 lime

Combine juice, sugar, tapioca and lime juice in saucepan; let stand for 5 minutes. Cook over medium heat until thickened. Pour into dessert dishes and serve chilled.

Yield: 3 to 4 servings

Marian Van Atta
Sapphire, North Carolina

Seagrape Jelly

To prepare juice, place washed grapes in large saucepot and cover with water. Simmer until grapes are soft. Pour through cloth jelly bag to strain. To make jelly, mix juice and sugar in saucepot. Bring to a boil and boil to 228 degrees on candy thermometer. Pour into sterilized jelly jars and seal.

Yield: 6 (6 ounce) jars

Marian Van Atta
Sapphire, North Carolina

Wild Strawberry Freezer Jam

2	cups sliced wild strawberries
4	cups sugar
1	package fruit pectin
¾	cup water

Combine strawberries and sugar, mixing thoroughly; let stand 10 minutes. Mix pectin with water in large saucepan, bring to a boil and boil for 1 minute, stirring constantly. Quickly add fruit, continuing to stir and cook for 3 minutes. Pour jam into sterilized glass or plastic containers with tight-fitting lids. Cover immediately. Let containers stand at room temperature for 24 hours, then place jam in freezer. Frozen jam may be thawed in microwave oven.

Wild raspberries may be substituted for strawberries.

Yield: 6 to 8 (6 ounce) jars

Jim and Ann Casada
Rock Hill, South Carolina

Strawberry Leather

5	cups strawberries
¼	cup sugar or honey

Place berries, 1 cup at a time, in blender and blend until smooth. Combine all berries with sugar. Line two 15x10x1-inch jellyroll pans with plastic wrap; eliminate any folds or creases and secure edges with tape. Spread strawberry mixture in the pans. Heat oven to 150 degrees, using candy or other thermometer at back on upper rack to confirm temperature. Place strawberry-filled pans in oven. Prop door open to allow moisture to escape. Rotate pans every 2 hours. Drying will take 6 to 12 hours. When leather is dry, remove from oven, invert on work surface and remove plastic wrap. Check to confirm dryness. Rewrap in plastic, rolling like jelly roll. Store at room temperature for up to 1 month, in the refrigerator for up to 3 months and in the freezer for up to 1 year. Send in school lunch pails and on backpacking or fishing trips.

Sylvia Bashline
Spruce Creek, Pennsylvania

Mother's Dandelion Dressing

When Sylvia Bashline was a child, dandelion green salad was served with the first pan-fried brook trout of the season. Best made with the very young dandelion leaves of spring, she finds lawns (organically grown and relatively free of animals) the most convenient spot for picking greens; pastures, fields and even vacant city lots are also good sources. She uses a narrow trowel, lifting some of the root with the leaves. Leaves attached to the crown are easier to handle through the first and second washing. For the last dunking, remove the leaves and wash individually in lots of cold salty water. Drain well and chill until ready to toss with dressing.

3	slices bacon, cut in 1-inch pieces
½	cup water
1	egg, beaten
2	tablespoons all-purpose flour
2	tablespoons wine vinegar
2	teaspoons sugar
	Salt and black pepper to taste
	Young dandelion leaves

Saute bacon until browned. Add water to bacon and drippings. Combine egg, flour, vinegar and sugar; mix well. Add to bacon and water, stirring constantly. Season with salt and pepper. Cook, stirring constantly, until dressing is thickened. Pour over greens just before serving and toss quickly.

Yield: 4 servings

Sylvia Bashline
Spruce Creek, Pennsylvania

Dandelion Vegetable

Dandelion roots
Water
Salt and black pepper to taste
Butter

Wash, peel and slice roots. Prepare like carrots, cooking in small amount of water and seasoned with salt and pepper. Drain and add small amount of butter.

Sylvia Bashline
Spruce Creek, Pennsylvania

Dandelion Blossom Stir-Fry

Dandelion blossoms
Salted water
Pancake batter
Vegetable oil
Salt and black pepper to taste

Wash blossoms thoroughly in salted water (salt draws out any insects). Drain thoroughly on paper towel. Prepare pancake batter from recipe or packaged mix. Dip blossoms in batter and fry quickly in oil in electric skillet heating to 365 to 375 degrees; blossoms will only require 1 to 2 minutes to cook crisp and browned. Drain on paper towel. Season with salt and pepper. Serve immediately.

Sylvia Bashline
Spruce Creek, Pennsylvania

Dandelion Coffee

Dandelion roots
Water

Wash and peel roots. Roast in a low temperature oven for 4 hours or until roots are brittle. Grind like coffee beans. Use in the manner of ground coffee except a slightly smaller amount of ground dandelions is required to equal the brewed strength of coffee.

Sylvia Bashline
Spruce Creek, Pennsylvania

Fiddleneck Ferns

Sam Roberson considers fiddleneck ferns "a very good spring vegetable for the backwoods chef", likening them to fresh asparagus. The cooking method can be used for another woods vegetable, the sea plantain or goose tongue, found on Alaskan beaches. The cooked plantain have a taste similar to young tender green beans.

	Young fern shoots, less than 12 inches long and partially curled
2	slices bacon, chopped
1	clove garlic, chopped
1 to 2	tablespoons water

Wash ferns, using brush to remove brown flaky coating (harmless but unappetizing); cut into bite-sized pieces and set aside. Saute bacon and garlic in skillet until bacon is crisp. Add ferns and water. Simmer, tightly covered, until ferns are fork tender, stirring occasionally to blend flavors. Serve like asparagus.

Sam H. Roberson
Lobelville, Tennessee

Goober Gulch Poke Sallet

Poke suffers too often from overcooking, according to Sam Roberson. Although the green does contain a poison which dissipates during cooking, Roberson has eaten it raw. This preparation eliminates the poison and intensifies the flavor. Poke grows freely in the wild over much of the United States where it tends to be underutilized and unappreciated. In Japan and other Asian countries, it's considered a vegetable delicacy.

2	slices bacon
	Poke greens, cut in bite-sized pieces
2	tablespoons soy sauce
2	eggs

Saute bacon until crisp, remove from drippings and set aside to drain. Add poke and soy sauce to hot drippings. Simmer, tightly covered, until poke is wilted. Drop eggs individually on poke. Cook, covered, until eggs are firm. Using spatula, cut around each egg and serve. Crumble bacon pieces over eggs.

Yield: 2 servings

Sam H. Roberson
Lobelville, Tennessee

Currant Punch

1 teaspoon ground ginger
1 teaspoon ground cinnamon
Dash of ground nutmeg
3 cups sugar
1 quart fresh currants
Water
Cracked ice

Combine ginger, cinnamon, nutmeg and sugar; add to fresh currants. Cook 15 minutes; strain and let cool. To serve, combine one part syrup and three parts water. Serve over cracked ice, if possible.

Betsy Neill
Brownspur, Mississippi

Campfire Peaches

This works just as well with apples, pears, apricots, and many other fruits of this type.

Peaches
Nutmeg
Cinnamon
Allspice
Lemon juice
Molasses or honey

Cut hole in peach from stem and carefully remove pit, without cutting all the way through the peach. Sprinkle cavity heavily with spices, and spread evenly with finger. Sprinkle lemon juice into cavity. Fill cavity halfway with molasses. Wrap peach in aluminum foil and heat by the fire until it feels soft and mushy. Peel foil away and eat with spoon, or serve over ice cream.

Robert Hitt Neill
Brownspur, Mississippi

Baked Peach Pudding

2	cups sliced fresh peaches
¾	cup sugar
½	cup milk
4	tablespoons butter or margarine
½	teaspoon salt
1	teaspoon baking powder
1	cup all-purpose flour

Topping

1	cup sugar
1	tablespoon cornstarch
¼	teaspoon salt
1	cup boiling water

Arrange peaches in bottom of a greased 8 x 8 x 2-inch pan. Cream butter with ¾ cup sugar. Sift together flour, ½ teaspoon salt and baking powder. Add to creamed mixture alternately with milk, in 4 or 5 additions. Beat until smooth. Spread batter over fruit. Mix 1 cup sugar with cornstarch and ¼ teaspoon salt. Sift over the batter. Pour the boiling water over all. Bake at 325 degrees for 1 hour. Serve warm with cream. This makes a pudding with a cake top and a thick syrup at the bottom.

Serves 6

Betsy Neill
Brownspur, Mississippi

"I caught the low, sweet music which belongs to nocturnal nature. I felt the magnificence of the purple hills, and of the clean moon riding above them. I was conscious of the beauty which belonged to the golden darkness. I felt that some Presence was near — Someone or Something that made the silence and the solitude complete."

Charlie Elliott

Watercress Sauce Verte

Watercress may have accompanied early immigrants to this country as a vitamin and food source for the long ship crossing. It grows well in the wild. Only the part above water will freeze and it will recover from low water levels and extremely cold weather. The prolific root system allows even a remnant to reflourish. Though treated somewhat as a joke in this country, watercress sandwiches are delicious. Sylvia Bashline suggests a 1:1 ratio of watercress sprigs with other greens in salads.

1	cup mayonnaise
¼	cup chopped watercress leaves
1	teaspoon lemon juice
	Salt and black pepper to taste

Combine mayonnaise, leaves, lemon juice and seasonings, mixing well. Chill for 1 hour before serving as sauce for cold or hot fish.

Yield: 1 cup

Sylvia Bashline
Spruce Creek, Pennsylvania

Watercress Sauce

2	tablespoons butter
2	tablespoons all-purpose flour
1	cup milk
1	teaspoon steak sauce
	Salt and black pepper to taste
¼	cup chopped watercress leaves

Melt butter in small saucepan. Blend in flour. Gradually add milk and cook until thickened. Add additional milk if sauce is too thick. Stir in steak sauce and season with salt and pepper. Blend in watercress. Serve immediately with hot poached, steamed or broiled fish.

Yield: 1 cup

Sylvia Bashline
Spruce Creek, Pennsylvania

Baked Stuffed Morels

The morel is considered by many to be the ultimate wild mushroom. Growing wild for about three weeks each spring and fall in burned areas, orchards and along spring banks, it resists cultivation. The morel has a smoky flavor; it has a hollow and pitted head with an appearance much like an enlarged peanut hull. Warning: Don't eat any mushroom you can not positively, absolutely identify.

	Morels
	Boiling water
1	clove garlic, chopped
1	tablespoon chopped chives or wild onion
	Salt and black pepper to taste
4 to 6	tablespoons white wine
¼	cup fine breadcrumbs
¼	cup grated Parmesan cheese
	Butter, melted

Quickly wash mushrooms to remove dirt from pits. Boil for 2 minutes and drain. Remove and chop stems. Mix stems, garlic, onion, seasonings and white wine in skillet or saucepan; simmer to blend flavors. Stir in breadcrumbs and cheese and mix well. Spoon stuffing into cavity of each mushroom and place in baking dish. Drizzle with butter. Bake, covered, at 350 degrees for 20 minutes.

Thomas K. Squier
Aberdeen, North Carolina

 "The farther ahead one fisherman gets, the quieter his partner becomes."

Charley Dickey

Side Dishes

The River

There's a fever raging,
in the hearts of some,
How long it lasts I do not know
nor when it first begun.

I only know I'm different
from lots of other men,
Where they fear to travel
I've already been.

The game I play is tough at best
the River has its terms,
Yet the love to hunt the mighty Miss
within my heart still burns.

There's other places one could hunt
easier to be sure,
Yet ole Miss is different,
she casts a magic lure.

Here's a truth that some folk know
my friends who know me well,
The River has me in its grasp
I'm caught within her spell.

And when I'm old and all worn out
and the River's just too much,
I'll quit a little earlier
And make it home for lunch.

The Mississippi River
holds me with its lore,
I know I'll hunt the River
until I hunt no more.

Bob Anderson

More Than You Ever Wanted To Know About Sourdough

Your sourdough starter, like a bucket of worms, is a living, breathing colony of little gilliwhicets shaped like teentsy footballs with swim fins and has to be treated as such. These little bugs eat starch, converting it to sugar, and pee alcohol, which can be converted to moonshine whiskey.

Sex, for the yeast bug, is an uninspiring experience. They eat and grow. When big enough, they divide in the middle, then both ends continue to eat and grow as separate individuals and so on, ad infinitum. Growth takes place best at 85 degrees Farenheit, slowing as the temperature drops, until activity all but ceases below 60 degrees. Rising temperature increases activity up to above 110 degrees, when the bugs become too frenetic, poop out and die. Under ideal conditions they will double every 30 to 45 minutes.

Millions of yeast bugs float around in the air and it is quite possible to catch a culture of your own by merely leaving an open container of growth medium standing around. This is sort of like going to the dog pound to secure a bird dog. You might come up with a humdinger but chances are slim. My own starter is a special strain, selected for its good qualities, as is a well-bred bird dog.

This starter dates back at least to the 1898 gold rush. It was given to me by Tom Landon, an oldtimer who acquired it from an elderly prospector whom he met while a "cheechako" or newcomer, about 1912. Tom lived in and around Fairbanks from then until World War II. He was a gold miner, big game guide, cut firewood for Yukon riverboats, carried mail by dogsled and such other things as necessary to make a living. When I met him, he was living in Tenakee Hot Springs and trolling for salmon in the coastal inlets of Southeast Alaska. Later he worked for the city of Juneau as a maintenance man. He was still there last I heard, going strong in his eighties.

Enough history. Now that you have the starter, what do you do with the damn thing?

What you have in the package is a puddle of starter mix, combined with straight flour, patted out into a cake and dried, putting the bugs into a dormant state. You break up this cake into a non-metallic bowl, since the acid produced by the bugs will eat into metal, as a couple of spoons I stirred with and laid in the sink without rinsing will testify. Also gives the mixture a metallic taste you can't get rid of.

Okay. Take a glass bowl, crumble in your starter cake, then add equal parts plain flour (not self-rising) and water. Use unbleached flour and unchlorinated water, if possible. I would suggest two cups of each as a fair-sized batch. Stir well, cover and let stand overnight in a warm spot until it gets bubbly and smells "sourdoughishly." Now it's ready to use.

First thing to take care of is your insurance. Take a small portion, maybe a quarter pint, package and store it in the deep freeze. Freezing stops all action. I've kept it for five years. This is for when you goof on the working batch; then you can pull out the frozen insurance and start again from square one.

Next, take out your working starter, another quarter pint or so, and pop this into the refrigerator. The chill slows the activity but doesn't stop it so some attention is needed. Do not seal tightly as the bugs will suffocate. Crack the lid a little. When left for awhile, a fluid forms on top which is highly acid and alcoholic and will kill the mix if allowed to build up. Pour this fluid off every week or so and add a little more flour and water to feed the bugs.

Now back to the bowl: with the insurance and next working starter taken off, the rest is yours and can be adulterated, mixed, mingled, etcetera, to your heart's content. I seldom bake bread but use the mix for hotcakes, coffee cake, blueberry muffins, whatever I desire. One friend of mine breads shrimp into the mix.

You can thin or thicken as desired, using flour and water. Add flavorings, fruit juices, nuts, berries, etcetera, to waffles or hotcakes. For coffee cake, throw in a cup of sugar, your flavorings and walnuts, molasses, coconut, berries, peaches or whatever; whip into a batter, throw the whole mess into a pan and bake, adding a range of toppings. Comes out a little dark and chewy, but awful tasty! My wife makes breads of corn, oats, rye or whole wheat with pumpkin, carrots, onions and other things for flavor. Experiment; just use common sense. The bugs don't mind; they just keep on growing!

Sam Roberson
Lobelville, Tennessee

Salami Stacks

1	(8 ounce) carton soft cream cheese
1	tablespoon horseradish
½	teaspoon onion powder
½	teaspoon garlic powder
16	slices salami

Combine cream cheese, horseradish and seasonings; blend well. Generously spread mixture between salami slices, forming stacks containing 4 slices. Cut each stack into 6 wedges and insert wooden pick for handling.

Yield: 2 dozen

Lynn Umstead
Greensboro, North Carolina

Cornbread Salad

6 to 7	cups crumbled cornbread
½	cup bacon bits
2	green bell peppers, chopped
2	medium-sized onions, chopped
2	medium tomatoes, chopped
	Salt to taste
½	cup chopped sweet pickles
1	cup mayonnaise
¼	cup sweet pickle juice
1	tablespoon sugar

Layer cornbread, bacon, peppers, onion and tomatoes in salad bowl. Season with salt and sprinkle pickles over vegetables. Combine mayonnaise, pickle juice and sugar; blend thoroughly. Drizzle dressing over vegetables. Chill. Toss lightly just before serving.

Yield: 12 servings

Mona Rollins
Clinton, Tennessee

French Onion Soup

5	very large Spanish onions, sliced very thin
7½	tablespoons butter, divided
2½	tablespoons unbleached flour or cornstarch
1	teaspoon sugar
1	teaspoon noniodized salt
1	teaspoon white pepper
6	cups water
12	beef-flavored bouillon cubes
1½	cups white wine
⅓	cup cognac
2	cups (8 ounces) grated Swiss cheese
	French bread, sliced and toasted

Saute onions in 6 tablespoons butter in cast iron Dutch oven over medium heat until onions are golden brown, stirring with wooden spoon. Gradually add flour. Stir in sugar, salt and pepper. Add water and bouillon cubes. Stir in wine and cognac, blending well. Bring to a boil, covered, then simmer for 4 to 5 hours. Preheat broiler to 550 degrees. Sprinkle small amount of cheese in ovenproof soup bowls. Pour in hot soup to nearly fill bowl. Place toast slice on soup, sprinkle additional cheese on toast and top with bits of butter. Place 4 to 6 bowls on baking sheet. Broil, 4 to 6 inches below heat source, until cheese is bubbly and beginning to brown.

Yield: 12 servings

James C. Wright, MD
Virginia Beach, Virginia

Ballard County Baked Beans

6	(14 to 16 ounce) cans pork and beans
1	(16 ounce) package brown sugar, divided
1	large onion, chopped

Combine pork and beans, brown sugar (reserving ¼ cup) and onion in 12x9x2-inch baking dish. Bake at 375 degrees for 1 hour, sprinkling with reserved brown sugar during the last 15 minutes of baking time.

Yield: 8 servings

Steve Vaughn
Paducah, Kentucky

Campstyle Cornbread Supper

2   pounds ground beef or veal
    Salt and black pepper to taste
2   large onions, chopped
1   green bell pepper, chopped
5   green onions, chopped
2   (8½ ounce) packages cornbread mix
1   (16 ounce) can cream-style corn
1   tomato, chopped
    Sour cream

Saute beef in heavy skillet, seasoning with salt and pepper. Remove beef and set aside. Saute vegetables in skillet drippings until soft. Spoon beef into ovenproof iron skillet or casserole. Place vegetables on beef. Prepare cornbread according to package directions; add corn. Pour batter on vegetables. Bake at 325 degrees for 35 to 40 minutes. Cut into squares and serve with tomato and sour cream.

Yield: 6 to 8 servings

Colette Moreau Lottinger
Luling, Louisiana

Duck Blind Apple

1   large onion
2   tablespoons butter
1   beef-flavored bouillon cube

Peel onion and cut slice from top to remove tough core. Place onion, flat surface up, on aluminum foil square. Place butter and bouillon cube on onion. Fold foil edges together to form tight packet. Place over charcoal bucket, propane heater or other heat source and cook for 30 minutes. Eat like an apple.

Yield: 1 serving

Howard P. Lindsey
Bowling Green, Kentucky

Butter Roasted Corn

6	tablespoons butter, softened
3	tablespoons minced parsley
1½	teaspoons salt
	Dash of paprika
6	ears corn, husked and cleaned

Combine butter, parsley, salt and paprika. Spread on corn. Loosely wrap each ear in aluminum foil, sealing tightly. Grill over hot coals for about 15 minutes, turning frequently. Partially unwrap and serve in foil.

Yield: 6 servings

John and Denise Phillips
Fairfield, Alabama

Stuffed Onions

4	large Vidalia or sweet onions
	Salt
1	pound ground venison, chuck, turkey, chicken or pork
1	envelope mushroom gravy mix
½	cup soft breadcrumbs
¼	cup milk
1	egg, lightly beaten
¼	teaspoon ground sage
¼	teaspoon black pepper
	Chopped parsley or parsley flakes

Prepare grill to produce medium-low coals. Peel onions and cut crosswise into halves; remove centers, leaving ½-inch shells. Sprinkle lightly with salt. Chop enough of onion centers to measure ½ cup. Combine onion, ground meat, gravy mix, breadcrumbs, milk, egg, sage and pepper. Spoon mixture into onion halves. Wrap in heavy duty aluminum foil, double folding edges to seal tightly. Grill for 35 to 45 minutes. Sprinkle with parsley just before serving.

Yield: 4 servings

John and Denise Phillips
Fairfield, Alabama

Vegetable Kebabs

2 red bell peppers, cut in ½-inch strips
2 small zucchini, cut in ½-inch slices
¼ cup vegetable oil
2 tablespoons lemon juice
2 tablespoons vinegar
2 teaspoons Worcestershire sauce
½ teaspoon salt
1 teaspoon Italian seasoning

Thread pepper and zucchini pieces on 8 (6 inch) bamboo skewers; place in shallow dish and set aside. Combine oil, lemon juice, vinegar, Worcestershire sauce and seasonings; mix well and pour over kebabs. Chill, covered, for 8 hours, turning once. Prepare grill to produce medium-hot grills. Grill kebabs for 10 to 15 minutes, turning and brushing occasionally with marinade.

Kebabs can be prepared in advance, placed in a covered plastic container in an ice chest and cooked at a campsite.

Yield: 8 servings

John and Denise Phillips
Fairfield, Alabama

Parmesan Baked Potatoes

4 baking potatoes
Vegetable shortening
4 tablespoons margarine
Salt to taste
Paprika
4 tablespoons grated Parmesan cheese

Prepare grill to produce hot coals. Rub potatoes with shortening. Loosely wrap each potato in aluminum foil, folding edges to seal. Place on grill and bake for about 1 hour or until tender, turning several times. Loosen foil. Cut a slit in top of each potato, checking for doneness. Place 1 tablespoon margarine, salt, paprika and 1 tablespoon cheese in slit.

Yield: 4 servings

John and Denise Phillips
Fairfield, Alabama

Indian Griddle Cakes

4	cups sour milk
1	large tablespoon butter, melted
2	eggs
1 ⅓	cups cornmeal
½	cup all-purpose flour
1	teaspoon baking soda
½	teaspoon salt
	Vegetable oil
	Salt

Combine milk, butter and eggs. Add cornmeal, flour, soda and salt; mix to form thin batter, adding additional ¼ cup cornmeal if necessary. Prepare griddle or cast iron skillet by rubbing with cloth saturated with vegetable oil and salt. Pour about ¼ cup batter on hot griddle to form each cake.

For camping, prepare batter and store in ice chest. Cook in skillet or on griddle over open fire or on campstove.

Yield: 30

John and Denise Phillips
Fairfield, Alabama

Grilled Garlic Bread

1	clove garlic
¼	teaspoon salt
½	cup margarine, softened
1	loaf French bread

Prepare grill to produce hot coals. Crush garlic with salt to form soft paste. Blend in margarine. Cut diagonal slices about ½-inches wide in loaf, leaving slices attached at bottom of loaf. Spread butter on top of loaf and between slices. Wrap loosely in aluminum foil, double folding ends to seal. Grill for about 10 minutes or until thoroughly heated, turning frequently. Bread may be heated in oven.

Yield: 10 servings

John and Denise Phillips
Fairfield, Alabama

Blueberry Muffins

2	cups unbleached flour
¾	cup sugar
1	tablespoon baking powder
1	teaspoon salt
¼	cup vegetable shortening
2	eggs, beaten
1	cup milk
1	cup blueberries

Sift flour, sugar, baking powder and salt together. Blend in shortening. Stir in eggs. Add milk, stirring just until dry ingredients are moistened. Fold in blueberries. Spoon batter into greased muffin tins, filling ⅔ full. Bake at 400 degrees for about 25 minutes.

Muffins freeze very well. Thaw, then reheat in microwave at high setting for 45 seconds.

Yield: 10 to 12

Pam Strickland
Natchez, Mississippi

Sour Cream Mini-Muffins

1	cup margarine, softened
1	(8 ounce) carton sour cream
2	cups self-rising flour

Combine margarine and sour cream, mixing until smooth. Gradually add flour, stirring until blended with creamed mixture. Spoon batter into ungreased 1¾-inch muffin tins. Bake at 350 degrees for 25 minutes.

Yield: 36

Elise Vachon
Marietta, Georgia

Great Pancakes

1   egg, well beaten
1   cup buttermilk
1   tablespoon vegetable oil
1   cup self-rising flour
1   tablespoon self-rising cornmeal
1   tablespoon sugar
    Butter
    Syrup

Combine egg, milk and oil. Add flour, cornmeal and sugar, mixing just until moistened. Preheat skillet with 1 tablespoon oil to medium hot. Pour 1½ heaping tablespoons batter into skillet; cook until lightly browned 1 side, turn and cook until browned on second side. Butter hot pancakes and serve with syrup.

Bob Kornegay
Blakely, Georgia

South Edisto River Red Horse Bread

½   cup self-rising flour
1   cup self-rising cornmeal
1   tablespoon sugar
1   egg
2   tablespoons vegetable oil
    Salt and black pepper to taste
    Milk
2   onions, chopped
    Vegetable oil

Combine flour, cornmeal and sugar. Blend in egg, oil, salt and pepper. Add enough milk to form a thick batter. Add onions and mix thoroughly. Drop tablespoons of batter into hot oil and fry until golden brown.

Yield: 24 to 30

Pat Williams
Santee, South Carolina

Beer Light Rolls

2	cups biscuit baking mix
2	tablespoons sugar
1	egg
¾	cup beer

Combine baking mix and sugar. Add egg and beer and blend with fork; do not beat. Spoon batter into hot greased muffin tins. Bake at 400 degrees for 12 to 15 minutes.

Rolls have a hearty texture and are absorbent, especially good to soak up red-eye gravy.

Yield: 8 to 10

Steve Vaughn
Paducah, Kentucky

All Purpose Meat Marinade

¾	cup soy sauce
¾	cup orange juice
¼	cup honey
¼	cup vegetable oil (for use with beef only; do not use on fowl or game)
½	cup chopped green or spring onion
4	cloves garlic, crushed
¼	cup thinly sliced fresh ginger root
2	teaspoons freshly ground black pepper

Combine soy sauce, orange juice, honey and oil; add onion, garlic, ginger and pepper. Pour over meat. Place in air-tight container in refrigerator. Marinate London broil for 12 to 24 hours, drain and grill. Marinate boneless chicken breast for 1 to 3 hours, drain and grill. Marinate pheasant, quail or Cornish game hen for 6 to 8 hours, drain and smoke slowly. Marinate salmon steak or fillet for 1 to 2 hours, drain and grill.

Yield: 2½ cups

Lynn Umstead
Greensboro, North Carolina

Cinnamon Rolls

1	cup boiling water
1	tablespoon salt
2	tablespoons shortening
1	cup milk
2	envelopes active dry yeast
5½	cups all-purpose flour, sifted
	Melted butter
	Cinnamon
½	cup sugar
	Powdered sugar
	Water

Combine boiling water, salt and shortening; stir until shortening is melted. Add milk. Sprinkle yeast over liquid and stir to dissolve. Add flour. Let mixture rise in warm place until doubled in bulk. Knead down and shape into a rectangle on floured surface. Brush dough with melted butter. Combine cinnamon and sugar; sprinkle over dough. Roll, jelly roll style, and press along seam to seal. Cut into slices and place in 13x9x2-inch baking pan which has been brushed with melted butter. Let rise until doubled in height. Bake at 350 degrees for 20 to 30 minutes. Cool in pan. Drizzle with glaze made by blending powdered sugar and water.

For camping, prepare rolls and bake until nearly done, then reheat and finish baking as needed. Or prepare dough, place in zip-closure plastic bag, store in ice chest and pinch off dough to make rolls. Or prepare at campsite, using camp oven that fits over campstove or Dutch oven set in open fire.

Yield: 48

John and Denise Phillips
Fairfield, Alabama

"When I feel the deep and unsatisfied inner yearning, it's time to pack my kit and slip away somewhere for a few days or weeks into a hidden remote corner of the globe."

Charlie Elliott

Sour Cream Yeast Rolls

1   (8 ounce) carton sour cream, heated
1   cup butter, not margarine
1   teaspoon salt
½   cup sugar, divided
2   eggs
2   tablespoons active dry yeast
½   cup warm water
4   cups unbleached all-purpose flour

Combine sour cream and butter. Mix salt with sugar, reserving ¼ teaspoon sugar; add salty sugar to sour cream mixture, stirring until dissolved. Add eggs. Dissolve yeast with reserved sugar in water, mixing well. Add yeast to sour cream mixture. Stir in flour. Chill, covered, for 6 hours or overnight. Divide dough into 4 portions and shape into balls. On floured surface, roll each into circle and divide into 12 pieces. Roll dough piece from center to edge and tuck corners under. Place 1 inch apart on greased baking sheet. Bake at 350 degrees for 14 to 16 minutes.

If in a hurry, dough can be used without 6 hour or overnight chilling. For lower fat and cholesterol, substitute margarine for butter, light sour cream for sour cream and egg substitute for eggs.

Yield: 48

John and Denise Phillips
Fairfield, Alabama

Sourdough Hotcakes

2   cups sourdough starter
2   eggs
¼   cup vegetable oil (optional)
½   teaspoon salt
½   teaspoon sugar
1   teaspoon baking soda

Combine starter, eggs, oil, salt, sugar and baking soda. Use like pancake batter, cooking on hot greased griddle or in skillet.

Sam H. Roberson
Lobelville, Tennessee

Alaska Sourdough Bread

2	cups sourdough starter
2½	cups warm water
¼	cup melted vegetable shortening
½	cup plus 1 tablespoon sugar
1	teaspoon baking soda
1	tablespoon salt
8	cups all-purpose flour

Combine ingredients in order listed, adding flour 1 cup at a time until no more can be worked into the dough. Knead on floured surface until smooth. Place in greased bowl and let rise until doubled in bulk. Knead down and let rise again. Punch down, knead, shape into loaves and let rise again. Bake at 350 degrees for about 30 minutes.

Sourdough is slower than yeast bread to rise. To hasten, mix 1 envelope active dry yeast to 1 cup warm water; substitute dissolved yeast for 1 cup sourdough starter.

Sam H. Roberson
Lobelville, Tennessee

Eye Opening Omelet

2	eggs
1	tablespoon milk
¼	teaspoon salt
2	teaspoons butter, melted
1	tablespoon chopped green chilies
1	jalapeño pepper, chopped
3	tablespoons grated Cheddar cheese

Combine egg, milk and salt; mix well. Place butter in 6 or 7-inch omelet pan; heat until butter begins to brown. Pour egg mixture into pan and cook over medium heat until partially set. Sprinkle with chilies, peppers and cheese; fold omelet in half and transfer to serving plate. Serve immediately.

Omelet is spicy hot so have cold beverage available.

Yield: 1 serving

Howard P. Lindsey
Bowling Green, Kentucky

Real Men Do Eat Quiche

1	unbaked 9-inch pastry shell
¾	pound bacon, cut in ½-inch pieces
½	cup chopped onion
1½	cups (6 ounces) shredded extra sharp Cheddar cheese, divided
6	eggs
1	cup half and half or milk
½	teaspoon salt
1	teaspoon cayenne pepper
⅛	teaspoon ground nutmeg

Using fork, prick holes in pastry shell. Bake at 425 degrees for 6 to 8 minutes. Set aside. Saute bacon and onion. Drain well and sprinkle in pastry shell. Sprinkle 1 cup cheese over bacon and onion. Combine eggs, milk and seasonings; mix well. Pour mixture over cheese layer and sprinkle with remaining cheese. Bake at 350 degrees for abut 50 minutes or until filling is firm.

Quiche can be prepared and frozen. Sausage, including summer sausage made from venison, can be substituted for bacon.

Yield: 6 to 8 servings

Howard P. Lindsey
Bowling Green, Kentucky

"Although the hunter is naturally a killer of wild game, nevertheless I have always contended that he is at heart the most valuable of conservationists. He knows the birds and animals as no mere 'nature lover' can ever know them. He is deeply and personally interested in the welfare and survival of game."

Archibald Rutledge

Log Cabin Lowballs

Citing the axiom, "necessity is the mother of invention," Sam Roberson offers this proof, created while mountain goat hunting. "We'd been running up and down cliffs all day in heavy rain," he recalls. Wet to the skin and bedraggled, the hunting party returned to camp about 10 p.m. Due to fly-in limitations, drink ingredients were scant; rum was available for emergencies and syrup for pancakes.

"A big mug of hot toddy after a long day on the goat mountain capped the day just right," he says, adding, "We got to using them for winter nightcaps at home. The nutmeg adds a little something."

2	tablespoons maple pancake syrup
¼	cup quality dark rum
	Hot water
	Nutmeg to taste

Mix syrup and rum while water heats and pour into mug. Add hot water to fill the mug and stir until syrup dissolves. Add nutmeg.

Yield: 1 serving

Sam Roberson
Lobelville, Tennessee

Friendship Tea

1	(3 ounce) jar instant orange juice powder
¼	cup instant tea granules
1 ¼	cups sugar
1	envelope unsweetened lemonade mix
1	teaspoon cinnamon
1	teaspoon ground cloves

Combine juice powder, tea granules, sugar, lemonade mix and spices; mix well. To use, mix 3 to 4 teaspoons mixture with 1 cup boiling water and stir until dissolved.

Yield: 48 servings

Elise Vachon
Marietta, Georgia

Desserts

Corduroy Coat

Her lover was a hunter;
But she hoped when they were wed
He would give up his childish ways
And be a man instead.
But when she found his hunting kept
Her man a little boy,
She gave him as a birthday gift
A coat of corduroy.

He wore it in the mountains,
In the marshes, on the shore;
It lost its color in the rain,
Briars its beauty tore,
And yet she wonderingly finds,
The shabbier it grows,
Its tattered charm superior
To that of costlier clothes.

Because it brings her snow and wind,
And hills of lonely height—
Her hunter setting forth at dawn,
And coming home at night—
The fragrant wilderness with him,
The wildwood's shine and shade,
It's taken on strange beauty that
Its maker never made.

Archibald Rutledge

Taste
the Flavor and
Spice of the Outdoors

No, I didn't step on a land mine, get shot in World War II…or crash my fighter plane…nothing that spectacular. In my youth I contracted polio which has limited my mobility to wheels, horseback and the backs of my buddies.

Outdoor writing friends have made it possible for me to live a full, rich life and know the rejuvenating power of God's great creation—the outdoors world of birds 'n' bees, flowers 'n' trees, fishes 'n' animals—all put for us to use, not exploit, is a powerful healer of mind and body. By making this outdoor world available to me, my friends added the flavor and spices that have made my life exciting and full of wonder.

As the former executive director of the Southeastern Outdoor Press Association, a strong regional outdoor writers group of which I was a founder, I became friends with many nationally-known writers. Each added his pinch of spice to make the living of my days exciting. In this capacity, my wife and I were encouraged to attend national conferences of the Outdoor Writers Association of America.

When we arrived in Snowmass, Colorado, a friend greeted me with the comment, "Good gosh, Tom! Who would have ever expected to see you here in the heart of the Rockies?" After the conference we made our way west and south to Moab, Utah, and saw Navajo women herding sheep and goats in Monument Valley and the Painted Desert.

At the Grand Canyon, I tried to visualize the powerful Colorado River eons ago as it carved its ever-deeping groove in the plains and marveled at His plan for us as I gazed at a layered cross-section of the earth in the colorful walls, buttes and plateaus of the Grand Canyon.

Because of the warm friendship of a host of men and women—the outdoor writers who took me out where I could hunt and fish, where I could shoot photos or shoot game, where I watched from our speeding airboat the rosy glow of dawn turn white egrets bright pink and, frightened as the sound of our exhaust reached them, taking flight in a great continuous wave as they left their roosts in Big Cypress Swamp. The "Sea of Grass"—the Everglades—could never be more beautiful.

We've shared the thrills of watching a flight of great white swans flying in the rosy fog twenty feet over my head at Lake Mattamuskeet, North Carolina, and taken Canada Geese in the nearby grain fields. We've seen roseate spoonbills searching for food on a Gulf Coast sandbar and sandhill cranes, a long way from their home in Nebraska's Snake River country, casually walking along the white sand beach, and an osprey feeding her young in a nest in a dead tree, and handfed a five pound sheepshead to a half-grown raccoon while we were fishing for snook and mangrove snapper around Florida's Ten Thousand Islands.

We've enjoyed the peaceful beauty while cruising the spectacular Blue Ridge Parkway, the Natchez Trace and the Outer Banks. The colorful woodlands, majestic mountains, the rolling hills and winding rivers all offer healing powers for our minds and hearts. The realization of our closeness to God there brings peace, renews our spirit and gives us an opportunity to redirect our thoughts and purpose of being uninterrupted by the noise of the mundane world in which we live.

A friend recently related how his collegiate son, in a rare extended visit for the holidays, came home weary of surgical pain and recuperation time, despondent, discouraged and blue. A recent fire had destroyed most of his personal possessions and each Christmas gift, usually a replacement (for that which was replaceable), reminded him of his loss. After Christmas, he and his father spent a few days in a remote woodland deer camp where they hunted, ate, slept and talked of things trivial and important.

Renewed in mind and body, loaded down with venison instead of problems, they enthusiastically returned to their individual pursuits knowing that God is in His Heaven and all personal priorities in place.

Tom Rollins
Clinton, Tennessee

Chocolate Applesauce Cake

Cake

1	cup sugar
1	cup applesauce
¼	cup butter, softened
1	egg
3	(1 ounce) squares chocolate, melted
2	cups all-purpose flour
½	teaspoon salt
1¾	teaspoons baking soda
1	cup water
1	cup chopped pecans

Frosting

6	tablespoons butter, softened
2	cups powdered sugar, rolled
3	tablespoons black coffee
3	(1 ounce) squares chocolate, melted
1	teaspoon vanilla flavoring

Combine sugar, applesauce, butter and egg; whip until frothy. Stir in melted chocolate. Add flour and salt. Dissolve baking soda in water and add to batter. Stir in pecans. Pour batter into greased and floured 10-inch tube pan. Place in cold oven, set oven temperature to 325 degrees and bake for 40 minutes or until wooden pick inserted near center comes out clean. Prepare frosting by blending butter, powdered sugar, black coffee and chocolate. Stir in vanilla. Frost hot cake.

Yield: 16 servings

Paul Jennewein
Wrightsville Beach, North Carolina

"I believe that more souls come to an understanding with their God in the wilderness than anywhere else on earth."

Charlie Elliott

Honey Applesauce Cake

For a truly "homemade" cake, use honey collected from backyard hives and applesauce made from apples and walnuts from trees in the yard.

Cake

½	cup vegetable shortening
1	cup honey
2	eggs
2¼	cups whole wheat flour
⅓	cup nonfat instant milk powder
1	teaspoon baking powder
1	teaspoon baking soda
½	teaspoon salt
½	teaspoon cinnamon
¼	teaspoon ground cloves
1	cup applesauce
1	cup raisins
1	cup chopped walnuts

Frosting

1	cup sifted powdered sugar
¼	teaspoon vanilla flavoring
1 to 2	tablespoons milk

Using electric mixer, cream shortening and honey at high speed until light and fluffy. Add eggs, 1 at a time, beating well after each addition. Combine flour, milk powder, baking powder, soda, salt, cinnamon and cloves; alternately add dry ingredients and applesauce to creamed mixture, beating well after each addition. Fold in raisins and nuts. Pour batter into greased and floured 10-inch tube or 12-inch fluted tube pan. Bake at 325 degrees for 35 to 45 minutes or until wooden pick inserted near center comes out clean. Immediately invert on wire rack and let cool. Combine powdered sugar, vanilla and milk to form glaze consistency. Drizzle over cooled cake.

Yield: 12 to 16 servings

John and Denise Phillips
Fairfield, Alabama

Plantation Cake

½ cup butter
1 cup sugar
1 egg
1⅔ cups all-purpose flour, sifted
1½ cups chopped nuts
½ teaspoon salt
1 teaspoon baking soda
1 teaspoon cinnamon
· ½ teaspoon allspice
2 tablespoons cocoa
1 cup applesauce, heated
1 teaspoon vanilla

Cream butter. Add sugar slowly. Cream until fluffy. Add egg and beat well. Add a little of the flour to the nuts. Sift remaining flour with other dry ingredients. Add flour mixture alternately with applesauce to creamed mixture. Stir in vanilla and nuts. Pour into a greased and floured bundt pan. Bake at 350 degrees for 40 minutes.

Betsy Neill
Brownspur, Mississippi

Buttermilk Pound Cake

3 cups sugar
1 cup shortening
5 eggs, separated
3 cups all-purpose flour, sifted
1 cup buttermilk
2 teaspoons vanilla
½ teaspoon baking soda
1 teaspoon salt

Cream sugar, shortening and egg yolks. Mix together dry ingredients. Add buttermilk alternately with dry ingredients to the creamed mixture. Beat together. Add vanilla. Fold in stiffly beaten egg whites. Pour into greased and floured bundt or angel food cake pan. Bake for 1 hour and 25 minutes at 325 degrees.

Betsy Neill
Brownspur, Mississippi

Old Fashioned Tea Cakes

1   cup butter, softened
2   cups sugar
3   eggs
2   tablespoons buttermilk
5   cups all-purpose flour
1   teaspoon baking soda
1   teaspoon vanilla flavoring
    Sugar

Cream butter until smooth. Gradually add sugar, beating well. Add eggs, 1 at a time, beating well after each addition. Add buttermilk and beat thoroughly. Combine flour and soda; add to creamed mixture. Stir in vanilla. Chill dough for several hours or overnight. Roll dough to ¼-inch thickness on lightly floured surface. Using 3½-inch cookie cutter, cut into circles and place 1 inch apart on lightly greased baking sheet. Sprinkle with sugar. Bake at 400 degrees for 7 to 8 minutes or until edges are lightly browned. Cool on wire rack.

To reduce fat and cholesterol, use egg substitute instead of eggs and margarine for butter.

Yield: 60

John and Denise Phillips
Fairfield, Alabama

Peanut Butter Bars

½   cup peanut butter
½   cup margarine
1½   cups sugar
2   eggs
1   teaspoon vanilla
1   cup self-rising flour, sifted

Combine peanut butter and margarine in bowl and place over hot water; stir until melted and blended. Remove from hot water. Add sugar, eggs, vanilla and flour, stirring until blended. Pour batter into greased and floured 13x9x2-inch baking pan. Bake at 350 degrees for 25 to 30 minutes. Cool before cutting into squares.

Yield: 24

Mona Rollins
Clinton, Tennessee

No Bake Cookies

2	cups sugar
½	cup milk
½	cup butter
¾	cup peanut butter or ½ cup cocoa
2 to 3	cups regular oatmeal, uncooked

Combine sugar, milk, butter and peanut butter or cocoa in saucepan. Bring to a boil, boil for 1 minute and remove from heat. Add oatmeal. Drop dough by teaspoonful on waxed paper. Cool until firm.

Package several cookies in plastic bags for hiking, camping or hunting.

Steve Vaughn
Paducah, Kentucky

Barlow Bottoms Chess Pie

Steve Vaughn describes this pie as "sinfully rich. This pie will make a misfire on a trophy rack seem like small potatoes." A hot cup of chicory coffee is a perfect complement to the pie.

½	cup butter or margarine
1 ½	cups sugar
3	eggs, beaten
1	tablespoon cider vinegar
1	tablespoon vanilla flavoring
¼	teaspoon salt
1	unbaked 9-inch pastry shell

Combine butter and sugar in saucepan. Cook over medium heat, stirring constantly, until very smooth. Remove from heat. Add eggs and mix thoroughly. Stir in vinegar, vanilla and salt. Pour into pastry shell. Bake at 300 degrees for 50 minutes or until knife tip inserted near center comes out clean.

Yield: 6 servings

Steve Vaughn
Paducah, Kentucky

Kentucky Chess Pie

1	cup firmly-packed brown sugar
½	cup sugar
1	tablespoon all-purpose flour
2	eggs
2	tablespoons milk
1	teaspoon vanilla flavoring
½	cup melted butter
1	cup pecans
1	unbaked 9-inch pastry shell

Combine sugars and flour. Add eggs, milk, vanilla and butter; beat thoroughly. Fold in nuts. Pour into pastry shell. Bake at 375 degrees for 40 to 50 minutes.

Yield: 6 servings

Steve Vaughn
Paducah, Kentucky

Chocolate Chess Pie

½	cup melted butter
¼	cup cocoa
1 ½	cups sugar
1	teaspoon vanilla
	Pinch of salt
3	eggs, lightly beaten
1	unbaked 9-inch pastry shell

Combine warm butter and cocoa, blending well. Add sugar, vanilla and salt; beat thoroughly. Add eggs and mix well. Pour into pastry shell. Bake at 425 degrees for 10 minutes, reduce oven temperature to 350 degrees and bake for 20 to 30 minutes.

Yield: 6 servings

Steve Vaughn
Paducah, Kentucky

Chocolate Chip Nut Pie

2	eggs, lightly beaten
1	cup sugar
½	cup all-purpose flour
½	cup melted margarine
1	teaspoon vanilla
1	(6 ounce) package chocolate chips
1	cup pecans or hickory nuts
1	unbaked 9-inch pastry shell

Combine eggs, sugar, flour, margarine and vanilla; blend well. Stir in chocolate chips and pecans. Pour into pastry shell. Bake at 325 degrees for 50 minutes.

If using a campstove, baking time may be shorter. Remove when crust is color of pecan shell.

Yield: 6 servings

Steve Vaughn
Paducah, Kentucky

Fudge Pie

¼	cup cocoa
¼	cup all-purpose flour
1	cup sugar
2	eggs
1	teaspoon vanilla
½	cup butter, melted
1	unbaked 9-inch pastry shell

Combine cocoa and flour. Add sugar, eggs, vanilla and butter, mixing well after each addition. Pour into pastry shell. Bake at 300 degrees for 45 minutes.

Yield: 6 servings

Steve Vaughn
Paducah, Kentucky

Fudge Pecan Pie

2   tablespoons butter or margarine
2   (1 ounce) squares unsweetened chocolate
3   eggs, lightly beaten
1   cup dark corn syrup
1   cup sugar
1   teaspoon vanilla flavoring
⅛   teaspoon salt
1   cup pecans
1   unbaked 9-inch pastry shell

Combine margarine and chocolate in top of double boiler over hot water; stir until melted. Combine eggs, syrup, sugar, chocolate mixture, vanilla and salt; mix well. Stir in pecans. Pour into pastry shell. Bake at 400 degrees for 15 minutes, reduce oven temperature to 350 degrees and bake for 30 to 35 minutes; filling will be slightly less firm at center than around edge.

Yield: 6 to 8 servings

John and Denise Phillips
Fairfield, Alabama

Pecan Pie

½   cup butter
1   cup light corn syrup
1   cup sugar
3   eggs, beaten
½   teaspoon lemon juice
1   teaspoon vanilla flavoring
1   cup whole pecans
1   unbaked 9-inch pastry shell

Brown butter in small saucepan; do not burn. Combine syrup, sugar, eggs, lemon juice, vanilla and pecans; mix well. Add butter and blend thoroughly. Pour into pastry shell. Bake at 425 degrees for 10 minutes, reduce oven temperature to 325 degrees and bake for 40 minutes.

Yield: 8 servings

James C. Wright, MD
Virginia Beach, Virginia

Quick Lemon Ice Box Pie

Steve Vaughn suggests this pie be saved "for the third day of roughing it. That's when tempers flare and taste buds begin to dull. This tangy taste treat will calm the crankiest hunter."

1   (6 ounce) can frozen lemonade concentrate
1   (13 ounce) can sweetened condensed milk
1   (9 inch) cookie crumb crust
1   (8 ounce) carton frozen whipped topping

Combine lemonade and milk; blend thoroughly. Pour into cookie crust. Spread whipped topping over filling. Chill before serving.

If outdoor temperatures are brisk, pie can be chilled without refrigeration.

Yield: 4 servings

Steve Vaughn
Paducah, Kentucky

Strawberry Pizza

¾   cup margarine, melted
1½   cups all-purpose flour
1   cup finely chopped pecans, divided
1   (8 ounce) package cream cheese, softened
1½   cups powdered sugar
2   teaspoons lemon juice
1   (8 ounce) carton frozen whipped topping, thawed, divided
4   cups sliced strawberries
1   (8 ounce) package strawberry glaze

Combine margarine, flour and ½ cup nuts. Press dough on large pizza pan to form crust. Bake at 350 degrees for 15 minutes or until lightly browned. Cool. Combine cheese, sugar and lemon juice. Fold in 1 cup whipped topping. Spread cheese mixture on cooled crust. Mix strawberries with glaze and spread over cheese layer. Spread remaining whipped topping over strawberries. Sprinkle with remaining nuts.

Yield: 12 servings

Phyllis Wade
Greensboro, North Carolina

Bread Pudding

6	cups stale French bread cubes
4	cups milk, scalded
½	cup melted butter
2	cups sugar
4	eggs
2	teaspoons vanilla flavoring
½	cup raisins
½	cup chopped pecans
¼	cup premium bourbon

Combine bread and milk; set aside to soak. Cream butter and sugar until smooth. Add eggs, 1 at a time, blending well after each addition. Stir in vanilla, raisins, pecans and bourbon. Add bread and milk and mix well. Pour into 3-quart casserole. Bake at 350 degrees for 30 to 45 minutes.

Yield: 12 servings

James C. Wright, MD
Virginia Beach, Virginia

Chocolate Moose

5	pounds chocolate candy kisses, foil removed and candy melted
1	moose (remove antlers)

Pour chocolate over moose.

Yield: Serves large crowd

Bettina Wood
Montgomery, Alabama

"We stumble on vast, comprehensible truths we did not know existed while we were in the world of men. We must be alone to find strength."

Charlie Elliott

Heavenly Hash

1   (16 ounce) package marshmallows, cut into small pieces
1   (16 ounce) can crushed pineapple
1   (16 ounce) carton frozen whipped topping, thawed
1   cup chopped nuts

Combine marshmallows and pineapple. Chill overnight. Just before serving, stir in whipped topping and nuts.

For camping, keep marshmallows out of sun and whipped topping in ice chest. Mix marshmallows and pineapple in 1-gallon zip-closure plastic bag; store in ice chest overnight. By second day, topping will be thawed; add to plastic bag and sprinkle with nuts.

Yield: 8 servings

Steve Vaughn
Paducah, Kentucky

Tropical Angel

1   rectangular angel food cake
1   (13 ounce) can mandarin oranges, well drained
1   (12 ounce) can crushed pineapple, well drained
½   cup shredded coconut
1   (12 ounce) carton frozen whipped topping, thawed
    Toasted sliced almonds

Cut 1-inch slice from top of cake and set slice aside. Scoop or pinch cake from middle of rectangle, leaving shell 1 inch thick on sides and 2 inches thick on bottom. Cut or tear cake pieces into bite-sized pieces and place in large bowl. Add fruit and ½ of whipped topping; mix well and spoon into cake shell. Place cake slice on cake. Frost with remaining whipped topping and sprinkle with almonds. Store in refrigerator for several hours before serving.

Yield: 12 servings

Lynn Umstead
Greensboro, North Carolina

Camp Caramel Apples

4 tart cooking apples
Melted butter
Brown sugar
Finely chopped nuts
Sweetened condensed milk
Finely shredded coconut

Spear apples through stem end with shish kebab skewers. Place on lightly greased grill or hold over coals, turning occasionally, until skins break and may be easily removed. Peel apples. Dip in melted butter, dip and twirl in deep bowl of brown sugar and hold over grill, turning until covered with rich caramel coating. Immediately dip tops of apples in nuts or milk, coat with coconut and hold over grill again until toasted.

Yield: 4 servings

John and Denise Phillips
Fairfield, Alabama

Boiled Cat

This unfortunately-named dish reputedly was a favorite with southern soldiers during "the late unpleasantries with our northern neighbors," according to Jimmy Jacobs. "One bite of this delicacy and you'll know why the Confederate Army was so mad it kept fighting for four years," he explains.

2 cups self-rising or all-purpose flour
1 cup sugar
1 cup water
1 cup sliced dried apples

Combine flour, sugar and water; mix to form large dough ball. Press to form a pocket in the middle of the ball, place apples in pocket and shape to enclose the apples. Place on a handkerchief and tie four corners to form a sack. Suspend on a string in a pot of boiling water over an open fire or campstove. Cook until dough is firm. Remove and let drip until dry. Unwrap, slice and serve.

Yield: 3 or 4 servings

Jimmy Jacobs
Mableton, Georgia

Raspberry Crepes

Crepes
1   cup all-purpose flour
2   tablespoons sugar
1½   cups whole milk
2   eggs
1   tablespoon vegetable oil

Filling
1   (8 ounce) package whipped cream cheese
⅓   cup slivered almonds, divided
1   (10 ounce) package frozen red raspberries, thawed
⅓   cup sugar
2   tablespoons cornstarch
2   tablespoons butter
2   tablespoons lemon juice

Combine flour, sugar and milk; mix until smooth. Add eggs, beating well. Mix in oil. Chill batter for 2 to 3 hours. Brush crepe pan with oil and place over medium heat. Pour 2 tablespoons batter into pan, tilting to form thin layer. Cook for 1 minute, turn and cook for 30 seconds. Repeat with remaining batter, placing crepes on towel to cool and stacking between wax paper sheets. If prepared in advance, store in refrigerator or freezer. To assemble, spread cream cheese on 8 crepes. Sprinkle with half of almonds. Roll crepes, jelly roll style, and place 2, seam side down, on individual dessert plates. Drain raspberries, reserving ½ cup juice. Combine juice, sugar and cornstarch in small saucepan. Cook over medium heat, stirring often, until syrup boils; cook for 1 minute. Remove from heat and stir in butter, lemon juice and raspberries. Spoon sauce over crepes and sprinkle with remaining almonds.

Yield: 4 servings

James C. Wright, MD
Virginia Beach, Virginia

"We Americans have an old saying…'If you want to know what sort of a fellow he is, take him on a camping, hunting, or fishing trip.'"

Charlie Elliott

Baked Alaska

1 (6x9 inch) fudge brownie
6 egg whites
¼ teaspoon cream of tartar
½ cup sugar
1 quart strawberry ice cream, slightly softened

Place brownie on baking sheet. Whip egg whites with cream of tartar until soft peaks form. Gradually add sugar, beating until whites are stiff. Place ice cream on brownie, shaping to form rounded mound. Spread meringue to cover ice cream. Freeze until ready to serve. Broil at 500 degrees for 2 to 3 minutes or until meringue begins to brown. Cut and serve immediately.

Yield: 8 servings

James C. Wright, MD
Virginia Beach, Virginia

Homemade Ice Cream

1½ cups sugar
Dash of salt
4 eggs, beaten
1 teaspoon vanilla
1 (13 ounce) can sweetened condensed milk
1 (14 ounce) can evaporated milk
2 quarts milk

Combine sugar, salt, eggs, vanilla, sweetened condensed milk and evaporated milk; blend well. Chill. Pour mixture into freezer cannister. Add 2 quarts milk and stir well. Pack freezer with ice. Add salt to ice and process according to freezer directions.

Yield: 3 quarts

Steve Vaughn
Paducah, Kentucky

Sunny Sherbet

2   cups sugar
2   cups boiling water
2   (3 ounce) packages flavored gelatin
½   cup lemon juice
1   cup cold water
4   cups milk

Combine sugar and boiling water; boil for 2 minutes. Stir in gelatin, lemon juice and cold water. Cool until consistency of syrup. Add milk. Freeze until edges are firm. Beat until fluffy. Freeze 2 hours or longer before serving.

Yield: 2 quarts

Elise Vachon
Marietta, Georgia

Microwave Fudge

1   (16 ounce) package powdered sugar
½   cup cocoa
½   cup butter
¼   cup evaporated milk
1   teaspoon vanilla flavoring
½   cup chopped nuts (optional)

Sift sugar and cocoa together into large microwave-safe bowl. Place butter and milk on top of dry ingredients but do not stir. Microwave at high setting for 2 minutes. Stir mixture, add vanilla and nuts and pour into 8x8x2-inch buttered baking pan. Cool and cut into squares (or eat with spoon before fudge is cool).

Yield: 25 pieces

Mary Walker
Scottsdale, Arizona

Pecan or Peanut Brittle

1   cup sugar
1   cup light corn syrup
2½   cups pecans or cocktail peanuts
1¼   teaspoons baking soda

Combine sugar and syrup in heavy saucepan or electric skillet. Cook, stirring constantly, until mixture begins to boil. Add nuts. Cook, stirring often, until candy thermometer reaches 300 degrees and mixture is golden brown. Remove from heat and stir in soda. Pour on buttered baking sheet and spread. Break cool candy into pieces.

Marjorie V. Walworth
Hephzibah, Georgia

Barbequed Bananas

This dish got the ultimate compliment when my daughters were in New Orleans once, and went to Brennan's Restaurant for their famous Breakfast At Brennan's. When the waiter served them Bananas Foster, B. C. took one bite and informed him, "Daddy's are better than yours!"

I think it's the mint.

3   bananas
     Cinnamon
     Nutmeg
     Allspice
     Brown sugar
     Butter or margarine
     Lemon juice
     Banana liqueur (optional)
3   sprigs mint

Peel bananas and lay on a piece of aluminum foil large enough to wrap them in. Slice bananas lengthwise, but not quite all the way through. Into the cavity, sprinkle cinnamon, nutmeg, and allspice, fairly heavily. Dot cavity with lumps of brown sugar and small slices of butter. Sprinkle with lemon juice. Sprinkle with banana liqueur. Lay sprigs of mint across bananas and close foil tightly, so that the package will retain the juices. Cook over low coals or on medium heat for up to 30 minutes, or until bananas are soft. Serve as is, or, for a real treat, over ice cream.

Robert Hitt Neill
Brownspur, Mississippi

Glossary &
Preparation Tips

Exile

So we were married, and I brought her home.
But after a little while she could not bear
The country that I loved. The big dark pines,
That kept on looming loftier in the dusk,
Gave her, she said, the shudders. The old owls,
The oaks' dim oracles made her afraid.
The sounds and silences that I could read
Were to her mind mysterious. I saw
The longing for the city and its ways.
Yet she was very gallant for a time.
But once she said: "If we stay here, I know
The grey moss will be growing on us both.
And you can't love it here as you love me."

So, from the old plantation cityward
We came, leaving the hollies and the oaks behind
To sentinel the home that we had left;
Leaving the wild birds singing on the boughs
Of blossoming dogwood, — how I envied them!
Leaving the hands in the cotton laughing,
The river flowing placid at our doors;
The sibilant whisper of the growing corn;
The hounds to hunt without my hearing them;
The jasmine and the woodbine, that would toss
Saffron and carmine showers, stayed in the air,
The wild azalea flaming in the woods, —
We unbeholding. And I left my gun
Hanging forever lonely in the hall.

About me now the buildings tower; the cries
Of many voices sound, but make no song
For me, a woodsman lost in Babylon.
And yet above me still the pine trees soar,
And still I hear the music of their harps.
I cannot see for all that I have seen:
The shadowy deer, furtively stealing forth
To roam the dewy country of the dark;
The old wild gobbler, that all night has slept
In starlight, in the shrouded cypress crest,
Sailing to the ground at sunrise in the wilds.
And sometimes, when the wind is in the south,
I know I smell the jasmine in the swamp,
And hear the mallards clamoring in the marsh.

Archibald Rutledge

Glossary
(or, "What the heck was that I just ate?!")

*T*he need for a glossary is clearly illustrated by the plight of the most delicious fresh water panfish: the Crappie. Yankees and other disadvantaged may pronounce this delicacy "Crap-pee," which hardly leaves one in a mood to eat anything, much less the fish in question. It's pronounced "Croppee." However, once we've cleared that up, the battle isn't even half over.

For Crappie are known by more names than any other fish, 55 according to authorities. I grew up calling them "White Perch" while my Cajun friends say "Sac-Au-Lait," meaning "bag of milk," a reference to its delicate white flesh. Tim Mead in North Carolina refers to "Calico Bass." Many fishermen call Crappie "Specks." Whatever nomenclature one uses to describe them in the water, all agree that "Delicious" is the common table term!

In addition, many wild meats are somewhat similar in texture and flavor, so that a recipe for dove, for instance, will usually work just as well for snipe or woodcock. When in doubt, trial and error based on the appearance of the meat works fairly well; just don't try a switcharoo on company the first time.

We covered "sploots," "gullops," and "dollops" in the front, so you don't have to worry about those anymore, right?

VENISON: This is deer meat, pure and simple, and around my house, the kids prefer it to the finest, corn-fed, Grade-A beef. Whitetail deer are the most common in the South, but most venison recipes work equally well with mule deer, or any of the other type deer found in other areas. Venison is a lean meat, and many cooks tend to cook it too long, drying it out. What fat there is on venison should be stripped off before cooking, as a general rule.

WATERFOWL: Self explanatory; fowl found around water. For our purposes, Ducks and Geese are discussed here, and many of the recipes for one will fare well with the other. A note of caution: some species of ducks will feed on fish occasionally, and their flesh will have a tell-tale smell, accordingly. Save the fish-eaters for gumbo, or in-laws you have little use for.

UPLAND BIRDS: These are game birds which don't swim for a living, though some are found close to water holes, like snipe. Wild Turkey is the largest upland game bird, some weighing in at nearly 20 pounds in oven-ready condition, while breasted Mourning Doves may have little more than two ounces of heft. Bobwhite Quail are certifiably the most delicious food to ever be served, when accompanied by dewberry jelly, with lemon meringue pie for dessert. Grouse and Pheasant, along with Quail and Turkey, are considered to be white meat, while Dove and Snipe are dark and almost indistinguishable from each other on the plate.

SMALL GAME AND CRITTERS: Everyone's favorites — Rabbit and Squirrel! In my opinion, Rabbit when prepared right is nearly as delicious as quail, and that's going some. Few people know that most recipes for tame lamb will work just as well on Rabbit, whether it's the ubiquitous Cottontail, or the larger Swamp Rabbit, also known as Canecutter in my neck of the woods. Grey Squirrels, or Cat Squirrels in some areas, are smaller than the more common Fox Squirrels, which may be colored (and thereby called) Red or Black Squirrels. Raccoons and Opossums (Coons and Possums) are more often hunted for their fur, but the meat, while fatty, is wonderful if prepared correctly. Froglegs got thrown into this category simply because they didn't fit elsewhere any better, and in my own opinion, that's Number Three on the Gourmet List, behind quail and rabbit. Woodchuck fits as a critter, since there is seldom a season on them. Ditto for Wild Hog.

CRUSTACEANS: I've often thought that the first man to eat a raw Oyster was either very brave, or very hungry. However, that's my Number Four choice. Saltwater shellfish like Clams, Crabs, Conch, Mussels, and Shrimp may also be found here, along with the latter's freshwater cousin, the Crawfish — a.k.a. Crawdad, Crayfish, and Mudbug.

FRESHWATER FISH: We've already talked about the Crappie (did you pronounce it right that time?). The flesh of Bass, both Smallmouth and Largemouth (also called Green Trout), is similar to Crappie, as is that of Bream — known by locals as Bluegill, Chinquapin, Redear, Goggleye, Red-eyed Bass, Pond Perch, and Lord knows how many other variations. Pickerel and Striper (Striped Bass or Rockfish) is also close to that taste and texture, so recipes for most of these species will usually interchange well. Trout — whether Rainbow, Brown, or Brook — is in a class by itself. Salmon is a sea-run fish, usually caught by sportsmen in fresh water, so its meat is different than any other listed here., Catfish are as familiar to every young fisherman as bream, and while so-called experts will argue all night about the virtues of Blue Cats over Channel, Yellow, Spotted, Mud, Gafftop, or Spoonbill where the table is concerned, it's all the same to me.

SALTWATER FISH: We've got just as many varieties here, and again, many of the recipes will interchange if the appearance of the flesh is similar. Nomenclature ranges widely; for instance, Sea Bass may also be referred to as Drum or Redfish; Mackerel may be Spanish, King, or Horse; Shark recipes work with most of that species, though larger ones tend to be tougher — and that word has a double meaning; if a Great White catches you before you catch him, you'll be the main ingredient in his recipe! In here we offer flat fish like Flounder and Halibut; Haddock and Tuna that hail from the ocean depths; exotic-sounding Triggerfish and Tautog; and well-known game species like Amberjack and the fatty Bluefish.

Preparation Tips for Both Field and Sink-Side

Wild Game and Fish differ from the standard supermarket fare, in that with the latter, someone has already done the dirty work. Steak comes in a neatly-wrapped package, and all a cook has to do is open same and pitch the meat onto the grill. With woods fare, the bloody part of the job is generally done by the sporting family, and often too little attention is paid to the steps that insure the taste. After a day on the lake fishing, most folks just want to hurry the cleaning in order to get to the beer and sunburn lotion, along with a hot shower.

Not trying to be indelicate here, but I have seen hunters bag a buck early in the morning, drag it to the road, load it into the jeep when it comes by at noon, hang it up when they get to camp; eat lunch; take a short nap; and then field-dress the deer in the middle of the afternoon. Then they give the meat away, declaring, "Venison tastes strong and gamey." Lordee, the finest grain-fed steer in the world would taste gamey if someone left the innards in it for eight hours after its death!

CARE IN THE FIELD

Get the innards out! This is known as field-dressing, or more coarsely, as gutting. Whatever one calls it, it is the most essential step to insuring the good taste of the creature one has bagged, be it deer, duck, squirrel, wood-chuck, or flounder. The decay process begins immediately after death, and the sooner the source of decay is removed, the better the meat will taste. In some cases, putting the deceased on ice slows the decay process enough to allow later cleaning without bad effects. This is an acceptable alternative with fish, for instance.

However, here are some quick tips to make sure your wild game suppers don't feature meat that tastes "wild" or "gamey."

DEER: Field-dressing doesn't have to be a long and messy process, if a good shot is made. Most of us can do it in little more than five minutes and only get one hand bloody. Briefly, follow these steps after the deer is down:

1. With a sharp knife, remove the testicles and cut free the penis and tube that leads back between the hind legs;
2. Cut around the anus and pull it out, exposing a foot of intestine; tie a knot in the intestine and insure that the bladder tube is cut free around the hole;
3. Slit the skin in a straight line from this hole up to the breastbone, being careful not to cut the intestines or belly;
4. Cut through the breastbone, all the way up into the neck;

5. Grasp the windpipe at the base of the neck, cut it loose above your hand, then pull downward. The heart and lungs are attached and will come out, requiring only that you reach into the cavity with one hand and cut around the diaphragm. When the diaphragm is loose, continue to pull downward, turning the carcass on its side, so that stomach and intestines come free as well.

6. Drape carcass over a log, cavity down and legs spread, to drain and cool.

7. Wash hand and have a cool one; you deserve it!

As long as daytime temperatures don't get above the low forties, I prefer to hang my deer (after the field-dressing) for two or three days before skinning and butchering. My son and I can perform these operations on a large buck in about three hours, including packaging the boned-out meat for the freezer.

Again, as a personal preference, we leave the loins whole, steak the hindquarters and large shoulder cuts, and use the rest for stewmeat, hamburger, and roasts. Drop a package of stewmeat in the crockpot in the morning, pour in enough of a good oil-base barbeque sauce to cover the meat, put the lid on, turn the pot on low, and leave the house for the day, because the aroma alone will cause you to gain five pounds before supper! Good and Easy!

Betsy likes to thaw her venison in salted water overnight, then soak the steaks in milk for a couple of hours before frying. For shish-ka-bobs or fondue, Italian dressing makes a fine marinade for the chunks of meat. Remember that venison is a lean meat, and don't overcook it!

SMALL GAME: Most small game animals are field-dressed just like deer, except on a smaller scale, of course. Leave out steps 1 and 2, since the parts in question are too small to fool with individually. Again, the sooner the better. Here are some tips:

Squirrels — skinning can be done quickly by cutting through the tail bone at its very base; carefully cut the two sinews just beneath the skin and expand the initial cut a half-inch down each hindquarter. Holding the squirrel by its hind legs, step firmly on the tail and pull slowly upwards. If you've done it right, the skin shucks off right over the head, and no hair will cling to the flesh.

Rabbits — The skin of a rabbit is notoriously thin, and makes possible an unusual method of field-dressing, insuring the taste and lightening the load. Hold the rabbit head-up and grasp firmly at the base of the rib cage; "milk" your hands slowly downward; when the intestines burst through the skin between the legs, simply "sling" the innards out.

Froglegs — a set of hedge clippers in the boat makes clipping the legs off easy, without even taking the frog off the gig.

Raccoons — There are several musk glands, easily found, on a coon. Remove these with a sharp knife before skinning.

BIRDS: Many hunters make a habit of breasting smaller game birds, such as doves, snipe, and quail, though my sainted Daddy would knock a knot on my head for breasting a bobwhite. To each his own, though.

1. To breast a small bird, break the wings up next to the body and discard wings; insert finger into the body cavity beneath the neck; gripping head and feet in one hand, and breast in other, simply pull the two apart. Remove remaining feathers and wash.
2. To breast a larger bird, lay it breast up and slice downward on each side of the breastbone with a sharp knife, keeping blade close to the bone; continue the cut across the bony rib cage and out to the side of the bird; remove remaining skin and feathers.
3. If breasting is not desired, or will not be done until later (note: in some states it may be illegal in the field), use a knife to slit the skin at the rear, reach in and pull innards out, and allow the bird to drain for a few moments.

CRUSTACEANS: Here again, ice is a necessity, and the shellfish should be cooled as soon as possible, if not kept alive. On crawfish, be sure to purge them while they are alive, like so:

1. Dump crawfish from container into large tub; fill tub with fresh water; add salt, the more the better. When the water turns muddy, drain it from the tub, rinse the crawfish, refill, and resalt. Repeat until salted water remains clear. You may then either cook or freeze the crawfish.

FISH: As noted, keep the catch alive on stringer or in livewell as long as possible. Store on ice afterward. A simple slice across the belly removes the entrails quickly.

Many fish have bloody streaks through the meat, easily visible after skinning. These should be removed with a sharp knife before cooking. Soaking fish in beer after skinning often makes the flesh firmer.

Some species, such as bass, have a flotation chamber that makes them easier to skin than scale. Cut down on either side of the top fin and pull it out. On a large fish, the top inch of skin will not be attached to the flesh, and can be easily grasped to pull the rest of the skin off, scales and all.

If filleting is desired, try an electric knife, even on smaller panfish. Again, scaling won't be required.

KITCHEN TIPS

1. Soaking meat of small game and birds in salt water for several hours after cleaning will pull dried blood clots, hair, or feathers out of the meat. Soak overnight, drain and rinse in the morning, and either freeze or prepare for the table.
2. As noted, soaking in milk tenderizes meat before frying.

3. The fat of wild meat is often distasteful; trim it off before cooking, as a general rule.

4. In addition to making fish filleting easy, an electric knife works well in slicing off deer steaks, once the meat has been severed from the bones.

5. Sear most wild meat quickly, or else add oil or liquids to keep from drying it out in cooking.

Index

OUTDOOR TABLES & TALES

Please send _____ copies of OUTDOOR TABLES & TALES @ $ 14.95 $ _____

Add postage and handling   @ $3.00 per book $ _____

Tennessee residents add sales tax   @ $1.23 per book $ _____

                                                               TOTAL $ _____

Make checks payable to WIMMER BOOKS PLUS.

Please charge to ☐ Mastercard   ☐ Visa Expiration Date _____

Card Number _____

Name of cardholder _____

Signature of cardholder _____ Phone ( )_____

SHIP TO: Name _____

            Address _____

            City _____ State _____ Zip _____

Mail to: Southeastern Outdoor Press Association
c/o Wimmer Books Plus
4210 B.F. Goodrich Blvd.
Memphis, TN 38118

Or Call: 1-800-727-1034 Or FAX: (901) 795-9806

OUTDOOR TABLES & TALES

Please send _____ copies of OUTDOOR TABLES & TALES @ $ 14.95 $ _____

Add postage and handling   @ $3.00 per book $ _____

Tennessee residents add sales tax   @ $1.23 per book $ _____

                                                               TOTAL $ _____

Make checks payable to WIMMER BOOKS PLUS.

Please charge to ☐ Mastercard   ☐ Visa Expiration Date _____

Card Number _____

Name of cardholder _____

Signature of cardholder _____ Phone ( )_____

SHIP TO: Name _____

            Address _____

            City _____ State _____ Zip _____

Mail to: Southeastern Outdoor Press Association
c/o Wimmer Books Plus
4210 B.F. Goodrich Blvd.
Memphis, TN 38118

Or Call: 1-800-727-1034 Or FAX: (901) 795-9806